Architecture for Achievement

BUILDING PATTERNS FOR SMALL SCHOOL LEARNING

ARCHITECTURE FOR ACHIEVEMENT *Building Patterns for Small School Learning*
Victoria Bergsagel, Tim Best, Kathleen Cushman, Lorne McConachie, Wendy Sauer,
David Stephen.

Architecture / Education / Small Schools / Community

ISBN 978-0-9796777-0-0
CIP data available

Book design by Sandra Delany

Funding for this publication was provided by the Bill & Melinda Gates Foundation.
The findings and conclusions of this publication do not necessarily represent the
official positions or policies of the funder.

Published in the United States of America by Eagle Chatter Press, LLC
Eagle Chatter Press, LLC, P.O. Box 24, Mercer Island, WA 98040
www.eaglechatterpress.com

Printed in Hong Kong by South Sea International Press, Ltd.

10 9 8 7 6 5 4 3 2 1

Architecture for Achievement

BUILDING PATTERNS FOR SMALL SCHOOL LEARNING

by Victoria Bergsagel

Tim Best

Kathleen Cushman

Lorne McConachie

Wendy Sauer

David Stephen

Foreword by Tom Vander Ark

EAGLE CHATTER PRESS

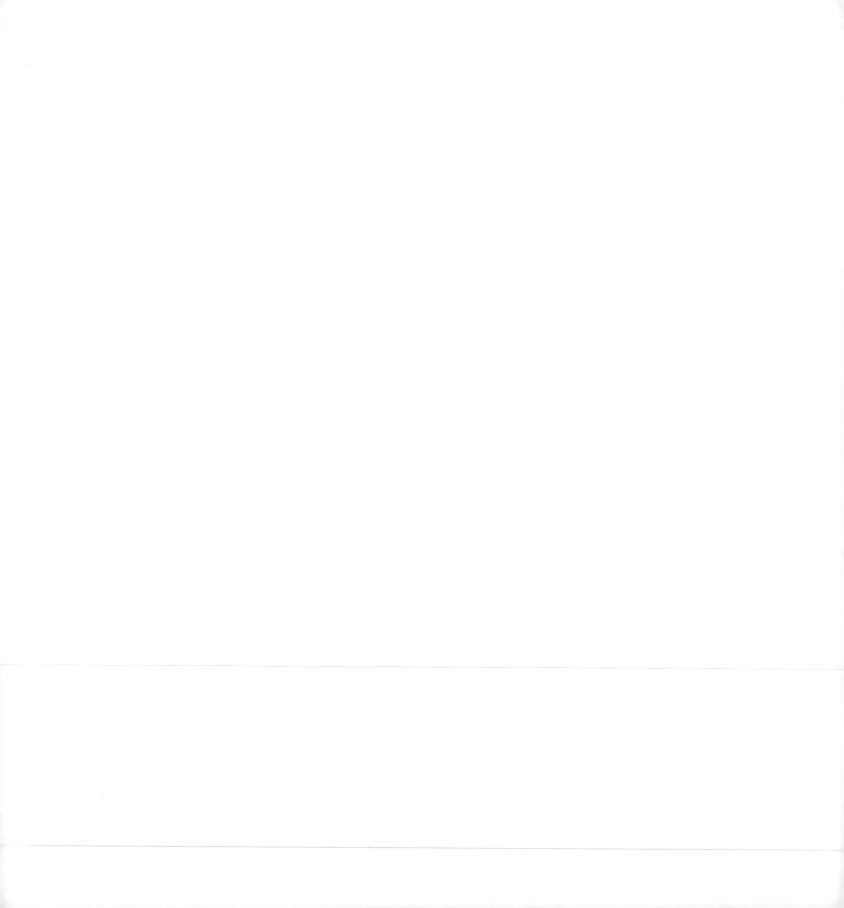

Thus, the task is not so much to see

what no one has yet seen,

but to think what nobody has yet thought

about what everybody has seen.

ARTHUR SCHOPENHAUER

Acknowledgments: The insight, knowledge, and dreams of Architects of Achievement's many partners have made this book possible. Thanks to our publisher, designer, and support personnel for their skillful expertise. Thanks to school faculties and leaders, students, parents, and community members who contributed to our understanding of how school facilities can best promote rigorous, relevant, and relationship-based learning. Thanks to the countless schools that have warmly opened up their doors to us – to photograph, to dialogue, and to learn. Thanks to the architects who, in working side by side with us on a variety of projects, have taught us a tremendous amount about school facilities planning and have graciously shared their drawings and plans for use in this publication. Thanks to courageous school superintendents for endeavoring – with us – to create personalized learning environments capable of their students' potential. Thanks to the Bill & Melinda Gates Foundation for their generous support. And thanks to the everyday heroes who, on a daily basis, devote themselves to bettering the lives of our nation's youth.

Contents

Foreword

By Tom Vander Ark

ARCHITECT LOUIS KAHN ONCE POINTED OUT that the original classroom was likely under the shade of a tree. Today, our nation's high schools – often housing upwards of 3,000 students – have fundamentally departed from this natural, intimate setting to become enormous and often impersonal complexes, recognizable to any airplane passenger at 10,000 feet. I do believe that extraordinary teaching and learning occurs in a variety of settings: in state-of-the-art facilities that support and encourage the teaching and learning occurring within them, and, conversely, in inadequate and in some cases dilapidated facilities.

Regardless of the setting, data from high schools across the country sadly remind us that, despite noteworthy efforts, student achievement remains stagnant. Approximately one-third of our nation's youth fail to graduate from high school, and just over 50 percent of African American and Hispanic students make it to graduation day. Of those who do graduate, far too few are prepared for the challenges of college and work. These statistics defy our nation's fundamental principle of equality and threaten its economic future. Fortunately, political, business, and education leaders are increasingly partnering with communities and organizations to improve high school education so that all of our nation's young people – whatever their background or economic status – have the opportunity to succeed.

The current failure of our nation's high schools rests upon a complex mixture of social, economic, political, and environmental factors. While this complexity can be daunting, researchers and practitioners agree that achievement increases when students are challenged, presented with authentic curriculum, and supported by both peers and adults in their learning environments. That's why the Bill & Melinda Gates Foundation has committed more than $1.7 billion to create new schools and redesign existing schools around these attributes; nationwide, hundreds of school districts are replacing the large comprehensive high school with smaller, more dynamic learning communities better capable of supporting student success. It only makes sense that this burgeoning high school reform movement be accompanied by smart design for educational facilities.

Research confirms that school facilities impact student learning. As school districts nationwide are projected to spend hundreds of billions of dollars on K-12 construction in the next decade, leaders have an unparalleled opportunity to use the facilities planning process to leverage educational reform. If we are truly committed to success for all learners, we must incorporate well-designed facilities into our reform agenda.

Such opportunities are all too often squandered. Many new high schools continue to be built using the traditional blueprint: long double-loaded corridors; uniformly-sized, forward-facing classrooms; departmental layouts; isolated teacher workspaces; and uninviting administrative offices. Nostalgic gravity – which pulls people back to what they know and have themselves experienced – and insufficient knowledge both stifle innovation. And the result is prettier – and perhaps smaller – school buildings, no more capable of bolstering student achievement than those they replaced. Most disturbing, these buildings often hinder the very rigorous, relevant, and relationship-based teaching and learning that their inhabitants have come to embrace as crucial for student achievement.

School spaces can function better and reflect what we know to be best practice. Facilities should support active, hands-on learning and performance-based assessment. Building design should invite both small- and large-group collaboration, while also providing space for focused, individual work. And ultimately, schools should stop getting in the way of exemplary teaching and learning.

The authors of this book have committed themselves to helping those involved with school design. I have known the lead author, Victoria Bergsagel, since she was a principal and I a superintendent in a large exurban school district in Washington state. She then went on to become the district's educational design director, spearheading the planning and development of award-winning schools. (Victoria's understanding of how people learn, honed as a director in a Seattle-based brain research institute, makes her a natural in developing exemplary school design projects.) In the process, she discovered that educators, school facilities personnel, and architects frequently struggled to effectively communicate to one another their nuanced thinking related to school design. Out of that need, Architects of Achievement was born, to help school districts, architects, charter organizations, and foundations think creatively about design solutions capable of fostering higher achievement for all.

Victoria has an uncanny skill for bringing insightful people together to work in an interdisciplinary fashion. The writing team she assembled for this project is no exception. In addition to herself, it includes a design expert proficient in technology and small schools theory, two innovative architects whose widely acclaimed school designs reflect a keen understanding of how architecture can foster improved outcomes, an accomplished author, and an educator well-versed in project-based instruction. Together they have woven a compelling narrative of how school facilities can play a critical role in educational reform.

This book builds on an established architectural principle – that good design can support the desired behaviors of the people who inhabit the space. It presents patterns for effective school design (replete with photographs, diagrams, and practical suggestions) and offers a common language for all those who are interested in developing more powerful learning environments.

Regardless of whether a group is designing from scratch, renovating existing buildings, or converting schools with few resources, this book provides a fresh way of thinking. The patterns included here provide educators with the voice necessary to describe how facilities can support their fundamental beliefs about effective teaching and learning, and they simultaneously illustrate for architects how school architecture can evolve to support new "best practice." Given their straightforward and clear presentation, the authors of this pattern language offer us the tools to dramatically redefine the role played by school facilities in the larger high school reform movement.

After decades of building institutional schools that often look and feel more like correctional facilities than places where amazing teaching and learning

occurs each day, isn't it high time that we do better? Shouldn't our schools –
like our homes, our cultural institutions, and our public spaces – reflect
the principles we hold most dear? This book is revolutionary in its ability
to help us achieve that goal. I look forward to a day when all students have
the opportunity to learn in places worthy of their potential.

*Tom Vander Ark is the President of the X PRIZE Foundation. Previously,
he served as the Executive Director of Education at the Bill & Melinda Gates
Foundation.*

Introduction

Redefining the American High School

T HIS IS NOT THE HIGH SCHOOL I REMEMBER," thinks a visitor stepping inside a small school in California. Upon entry, she is greeted not by security guards but by a helpful receptionist at a low-profile desk. A student quickly notices the visitor and, rather than turning away, engages her in conversation. "Can I help you?" another student inquires, introducing himself and asking about the purpose of her visit. Students circulate in wide, open hallways, carrying not hall passes but projects in their hands. Teachers and students collaborate in comfortable seating at round tables, rather than in crowded classrooms with desks in rows. Student art and academic work cover the walls, not rules, regulations, and photographs from graduating classes long past. Technology is mobile and ubiquitous rather than isolated in computer labs. Gone are the dirty, poorly lit hallways of the past; this campus is clean, with abundant natural light. Students and teachers eat lunch together rather than in a segregated cafeteria and faculty room. And in this welcoming setting, students are engaged in learning, not just passing the time.

This school reflects new patterns of teaching and learning that have taken hold in urban, rural, and suburban districts nationwide. In such schools, teachers have the opportunity to know students well, coaching their development in ways that intertwine the academic and the personal. They take learning into the field, prompting students to ask questions and seek answers based on investigation and observation. They challenge students to demonstrate their understanding in public presentations. They teach communication comprehensively, encouraging students to express themselves and their learning in a variety of forms. And they are on the rise, as state, district, and school leaders, with the support of philanthropic organizations, grow increasingly determined to remake the American high school.

New educational approaches require new architectural patterns to support them, which challenge the familiar high school design patterns passed down through generations. We can see some of those old patterns in the academic tactics (such as workbook drills or multiple-choice tests) that schools use to command and control large groups of students. But they also show up as recurring elements in school architecture. The confining classrooms, the rows of desks facing front, the institutional corridors – all reinforce the message that high school is a place where young people comply with authorities who dispense information, not a place where they actively construct knowledge and create meaning.

New educational approaches require new architectural patterns to support them, which challenge the familiar high school design patterns passed down through generations.

We must confront these common design assumptions embedded in the place we call school. Our nation is in the midst of the biggest school building boom in its history, which shows little sign of slowing anytime soon. That investment, concurrent with larger trends in high school reform, should prompt serious thought about the opportunity to build stronger bridges between the worlds of education, community, and architecture.

Architects of Achievement, our team of architects, educators, community activists, and communication experts, focuses on such bridge-building.

As we help schools start up, grow, or reconfigure, we notice that the physical spaces they occupy have enormous power to either propel or blunt their efforts to transform teaching and learning. While strong, innovative programs can succeed in spite of a building's architecture, we have found that the marriage of form and function can enhance and further shape a school's learning culture. This book provides the design tools to transform school buildings into more powerful places of learning.

A 'Pattern Language' for School Design

As we work with districts nationwide to provide tools related to facilities reform, we often turn to the work of Christopher Alexander and his colleagues, who described an inspiring approach to design in the now classic *Pattern Language: Towns, Buildings, Construction*. That book rests on the premise that when we create spaces in which to live and work we are solving human problems that recur in our environments.

Once we understand how architecture gives form to the patterns by which we live, we begin to see how a school's spaces can also express and influence its philosophy. The very process of designing such spaces prompts us to reflect more deeply about what schools stand for, and how they interact within their larger environment. "When you build a thing you cannot merely build that thing in isolation," Alexander writes, "but must also repair the world around it, and within it." His statement deeply resonates with the challenges school people face as they try, for the sake of future generations, to reshape public policies and attitudes about high school education.

"When you build a thing you cannot merely build that thing in isolation," Alexander writes, "but must also repair the world around it, and within it."

Taken together, architectural patterns create an entire language with which we can express things that matter – just as musical patterns, or the patterns of dance, often convey deep truths that words sometimes cannot. And although such a "pattern language" articulates universal truths, each person or group may construct its language and grammatical rules differently. Alexander's classic "pattern language" consists of 253 patterns that apply to a very wide range of issues, from "the distribution of towns" to "things from your life." Yet he suggests that others take his ideas as a point of departure in developing their own languages, as they work out what they want to say about their needs. Here we present twenty-six design patterns for those thinking about the building needs of dynamic schools and, more specifically, of small schools and small learning communities.

Guiding Principles for Student Success

Prior to developing our "pattern language," our team has collectively spent years studying and observing attributes of successful schools. Our research and experience resulted in the development of guiding principles for smart small school design. These principles, around which we have organized our patterns, must permeate all educational and design aspects of a learning environment.

Personalized. Historically, high schools have been places where anonymity reigns. Students are identified by numbers and teachers see upwards of 150 learners in any school day. Not surprisingly, research argues that such impersonal environments discourage student success. Students achieve at higher levels when they are known well by adults at school. As trusting student-adult relationships develop, learning becomes increasingly individualized and students receive the requisite support to achieve at levels not previously attainable.

Learning-focused. Statistics affirm that a high school diploma is no longer sufficient to earn a living family wage. In order to succeed in the workplace or in institutions of higher learning, high school students must be literate and mathematically competent, adept problem-solvers, and effective written and oral communicators. Our society and economy can no longer afford high schools that promote students to a higher level merely for showing up. Rather, our schools must commit to a challenging, engaging curriculum for all learners.

Collaborative. Historically, high schools have isolated their inhabitants. Teachers plan lessons and instruct classes behind closed doors, with very little collegial interaction. Students are asked to sit quietly at their desks, speaking to their teachers or peers only when directed. Administrators remain chained to their desks, so busy with bureaucracy that they rarely spend time in hallways and classrooms. Parents come to school only when problems arise. Effective schools defy such isolation, insisting that students, adults, family, and community work together to foster student achievement.

Community-connected. A high school, particularly one in a suburban or rural setting, was once the center and pride of its community. Increasingly, however, high schools are institutionalized and shut off. Breaking down the walls between school and community is vital to school success. Community connections can authenticate the curriculum and lead to higher student engagement. In turn, good schools can also revitalize communities.

Adaptable and flexible. Too many high schools teach students in the same outmoded buildings, using the curriculum of generations long past. And yet our world has changed in drastic ways. School design must acknowledge the rapid pace of change, creating structures both flexible in the short run and adaptable in the long run. Only by so doing will our nation avoid repeating the situation in which we now find ourselves – a secondary school system that no longer meets the needs of its learners.

Our nation, our states, and our school districts must make a priority of creating personalized, learning-focused, collaborative, and community-connected school buildings that can flex and adapt in both the short and long term. That investment will pay rich dividends as all students – regardless of their economic or ethnic background – flourish and achieve.

Why Small High Schools?

A large, comprehensive high school structure cannot embrace these guiding principles. Such schools are inherently impersonal. They rely on learning tracks that segregate students rather than exposing all to a rigorous curriculum. They isolate teachers and are themselves isolated from the surrounding community. And they are slow to change. Student achievement, not surprisingly, has suffered. Our nation's high school graduation rates hover around 70 percent, and closer to 50 percent for African-American and Hispanic youth.

Small high schools, on the other hand, have decisively shown their effectiveness by both qualitative and quantitative measures, particularly for students historically underserved. They bring significantly more students to graduation

Our nation, our states, and our school districts must make a priority of creating personalized, learning-focused, collaborative, and community-connected school buildings that can flex and adapt in both the short and long term.

than do their much larger counterparts. Teachers in these settings are collaborating to improve their professional practices and adapt them to students' individual needs. Students, teachers, and parents form closer bonds; schools' relationships with their communities thrive. As they break down the isolation and anonymity of the conventional high school experience, these small schools are helping more students find success in college, work, and the community.

Recognizing the success of grouping students in smaller numbers, districts around the country are endeavoring to create smaller learning environments within their systems. Some have the luxury of creating small schools from scratch. Such schools may be housed in new buildings, or in existing buildings adapted for their use. Some join together to form a village of small schools. Others are reconstituting and reorganizing comprehensive high school buildings into multiplexes of small, autonomous schools or small learning communities.

Regardless of the strategy selected to "right-size" their high schools, educators, school building committees, and architects must first understand and articulate the connections between the educational programs they envision and the architectural spaces in which they will evolve. The building alone cannot bring about the changes hoped for – but the building can certainly support the change, by encouraging more personalized and powerful teaching and learning.

The building alone cannot bring about the changes hoped for – but the building can certainly support the change, by encouraging more personalized and powerful teaching and learning.

Surfacing Assumptions

If school buildings are to encourage transformational change, we must call into question the comprehensive high school experience, so deeply embedded in the American psyche. Otherwise, nostalgic thinking for "what was" exerts a gravitational pull back to the familiar. For instance, when one assumes that a high school must provide a comprehensive array of services, extracurricular activities, facilities, and programs, the traditional gyms, fields, libraries, swimming pools, and auditoriums tend to drive up the size of the school to justify a perceived economy of scale.

We call into question such assumptions.

. . . nostalgic thinking for "what was" exerts a gravitational pull back to the familiar.

Communities can enter the world of secondary school reform from many points, finding many ways to get "from here to there" as they work to design

more powerful places for learning. Which activities and amenities to offer in school buildings will therefore be complex decisions, involving cost, focus (intentional and unintentional), facility availability, community assets, culture, and instructional practices. The conclusions that planners reach regarding what paths to take – to meet various needs, in various ways, for various learners – inevitably reflect community values, as well as shaping the dreams and aspirations of the next generation.

We believe that success in overcoming the nostalgic gravity of the comprehensive high school will rest on four critical factors: the engagement of the school's community in meaningful ways; the courage, skill, and fortitude of its leaders; effective professional development for teachers; and, finally, the design of facilities in which these new small high school environments will carry out their ideals and goals. That last condition affirms our purpose: providing design tools to tailor buildings so that they meet the needs of all learners.

How to Use This Book

This book offers school people and architects a way to match educational ideas with buildings that powerfully support them. To encourage active inquiry among teenagers, for instance, how should we configure a school's learning spaces? What acoustical demands or display requirements or storage needs might arise when we emphasize hands-on projects in the curriculum? From that one principle, we can see patterns of all kinds begin to take their place in our new language. In turn, the language helps us bring our principles into more coherent action.

Architecture, like language, is not a linear process, and we offer this book to prompt new ideas, not to prescribe them.

Architecture, like language, is not a linear process, and we offer this book to prompt new ideas, not to prescribe them. We see our 26 small school patterns as a starting point. Many other patterns certainly exist, and we hope readers will suggest them as this conversation evolves – bearing in mind that powerful pattern languages are in harmony with geography, climate, context, and the culture of place.

Our patterns are organized by the five principles outlined above, reinforcing the point that architectural choices – like all choices made about learning environments – must aim to help all students succeed. Like Christopher Alexander, we begin each pattern description with a principle and end it with a suggestion for practice. And, like him, we suggest cross-references among patterns, and their combination, creating a network for readers to use as they shape and organize their ideas into the design for a small school or campus of small learning communities.

We take our illustrations largely from our own practice and experience. Though that limits their geographical range, we hope they encompass a broad scope of possibilities, and encourage dialogue about how to encourage more equitable and personalized learning environments better suited to meet the needs of all learners. Our examples focus primarily on secondary schools because we think they offer our nation some of its greatest educational challenges.

A healthy debate is warranted and innovation is essential if we intend to meet the current and future needs of all learners.

Since one size never fits all, we hope our ideas help school systems become systems of schools that provide a broader range of options for students and their families. We hope to  encourage a dialogue that focuses on supporting the rich diversity of learning needs in our schools today. A healthy debate is warranted and innovation is essential if we intend to meet the current and future needs of all learners.

We intend this book not as a how-to manual, but as a way to build bridges linking architects, educators, administrators, students, community members, contractors, and trades people in the essential conversations that precede and accompany a building project. Our book contains no easy answers; instead, it aims to ask better questions. In the spirit of small schools, we hope those questions will recur and deepen as the reader dips again and again into these patterns, learning and using their language until our practice – of architecture and of education – begins to create new meanings, and new places of learning where all of us will thrive.

MULTIPLE POINTS OF ENTRY

Architecture for Achievement: Building Patterns for Small School Learning provides models and a common language for anyone interested in thinking about physical spaces that best support learning. These patterns should serve two different groups involved in school facilities: facilities planners, architects, and builders; and the educators and learners who call on them. Both parties can use this common pattern language to increase communication and understanding as they design, build, and renovate school buildings. The public at large constitutes a third, broader audience, of community members, policymakers, and business people interested in creating environments that support learning.

Who should use this book:

- Teachers and staff
- School building committees
- Architects
- Administrators
- Parents
- Students
- School boards
- Contractors
- Engineers
- Trades people
- Community planners and commissions
- City and county councils
- Citizens advisory committees
- Transportation planners
- Interior and industrial designers
- Furniture designers

Adaptable and Flexible   *Community-Connected*

Personalized

Learning-Focused

COLLABORATIVE

The Patterns

Personalized

Sustained relationships among students and adults are promoted. Personalized learning environments offer the opportunity for all students to be known well and encouraged academically.

1. Human Scale

Small details, such as doors scaled to the size of a school's learners, suggest that students and their comfort are a central priority.

At left: Hallway width, ceiling height, warm light, and vibrant color all humanize this middle school's corridor.

A small school's buildings can embody the belief that learning happens best on a human scale. Students and adults at successful small schools know each other well – as they go about their academic pursuits, they are continually working in relationship with each other. They need places that reflect and support that priority, creating a collegial family atmosphere whose scale suits its purpose of thoughtful interactions.

Students at a small school often regard it as a safe haven as well as a place to learn. A nurturing climate develops when the school's program and its facilities encourage personal interactions rather than focusing on people management and control. A large and monolithic school building sends the opposite message; those within it can feel its impersonal character and may even act it out in unconscious behavior patterns.

Educators and architects can address this anonymity by making buildings on a more human scale. Rather than housing 1,000 students together in a comprehensive school, for example, a new school might create a village-like campus of distinct small learning communities in separate buildings with

The brick buildings on this campus of four small schools reflect the residential scale of the surrounding urban neighborhood.

shared spaces including a gym, a theater, or a media center. A lively street pattern might link the various buildings with other site amenities such as plazas, outdoor learning areas, parking, and other community resources.

Even a large new building can evoke the feeling of distinct neighborhoods within a village, rather than a factory-style institution, by using an assemblage of forms and volumes that vary in size and character. Instead of casting one huge roof over everything, for example, an architect could break up the building's mass by designing a variety of spaces with varying heights, rooflines, materials, ornamentation, and focal elements. Breaking up the elements of the learning community allows each to have its own form and size, a "neighborhood" that conveys respect for the differences among learners and their interests and pursuits.

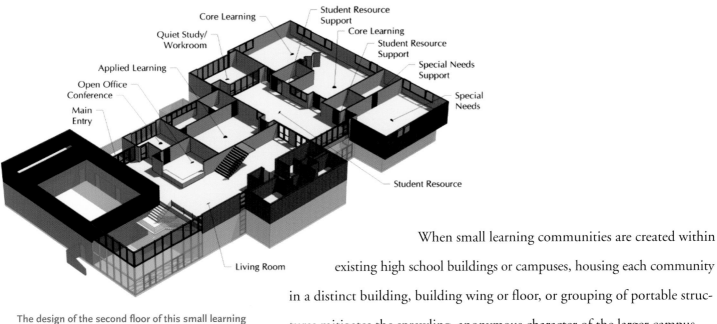

Core Learning

Quiet Study/
Workroom

Applied Learning

Open Office
Conference

Main
Entry

Student Resource
Support

Core Learning

Student Resource
Support

Special Needs
Support

Special
Needs

Student Resource

Living Room

The design of the second floor of this small learning community enables the building to meet individual student needs. Varied spaces, accessible resources, and generous gathering spaces allow learning to remain the priority.

When small learning communities are created within existing high school buildings or campuses, housing each community in a distinct building, building wing or floor, or grouping of portable structures mitigates the sprawling, anonymous character of the larger campus. Close study of a campus map typically reveals natural locations for multiple learning communities.

Sometimes a small learning community includes as many as 450 to 600 students. In that case, housing students in even smaller clusters (or "families") of 100 to 150, with interdisciplinary teams situated in adjacent classrooms, can establish a culture where students are better known and supported.

The places where learning spaces intersect or join can themselves hold interest, in much the same way that the popular gathering areas of cities often evolve over time without planning. In a multiplex setting, for instance, the space where a library connects to a classroom wing can turn into a crossroads where people meet and work or just hang out.

From its very conceptual stages,
this school's layout was intended
to embrace all learners.

▶ **IN PRACTICE**

Whether building a small school, creating a multiplex of several small schools, or converting a large school into small learning communities, design your school's physical setting on a scale that permits all the participants in a learning community to know each other well. Avoid elements that treat community members as an undifferentiated crowd. Whenever possible, create interest and variety by breaking down large masses and using varied forms and volumes.

2. Greeting and Gatekeeping

This small school's appealing reception kiosk provides a gracious first point of contact for all who enter.

Promptly upon entering a small school, people like to encounter a reception point where someone greets them in a warm yet professional manner. The design of this area can convey the sense that they have crossed the threshold from the larger world into a place characterized by a purposeful knowing of every person there. This serves not only to render the school secure, but also to welcome people into a community of learning where others respect their identities and their work.

In the professional business environment, we have grown used to formal welcome areas, but they rarely exist in school buildings. Instead, many schools guard their entrances with mechanisms like metal detectors or video cameras that convey impersonal suspicion. Once past the security point, outsiders and even students often encounter a person situated behind a tall, imposing counter rather than someone who greets them in a professional and respectful manner. To find the offices of teachers or administrators, they often must navigate a confusing maze of hallways.

As visitors enter an educational complex, someone can greet them and encourage them to take a seat, offer assistance, and direct them to the various small learning communities on campus.

In contrast, a small school's design can use its gatekeeping point to make clear its priority of knowing every member of its community. In a larger building shared by several small schools, a cordial person might staff a central reception point for identification and sign-in, directing people to smaller greeting points for each small school. Such greeting points are best placed directly off the larger school's organizing spine or quad. A certain formality to the central entrance system lends a sense that a code of respectful behavior prevails in the community as a whole; as a person proceeds into the small school, the atmosphere may modulate into a more informal tone.

For instance, six small schools now share a classic red brick building that once housed a comprehensive high school on the East Side of Manhattan. In its spacious lobby, security officers greet every visitor from behind a low sign-in table. Up the stairs to the left, visitors to one 120-student high school immediately encounter students who graciously greet and escort them to the office. Everyone shares in the work of making this small school with its informal atmosphere a safe, personal, and respectful place.

A small school's welcome point can also give entrants an immediate sense that they belong in the work of this learning community. If it provides a place to sit down, outsiders might observe the flow of students and adults or pause to converse with someone. If it offers a sightline into areas of study, conference, or exhibition, they might more easily get their bearings, finding

This reception area, at the entrance to a small learning community on a large high school campus, stands in sharp contrast to the oft-imposing front office counter at many high schools. It invites conversation and communicates welcome.

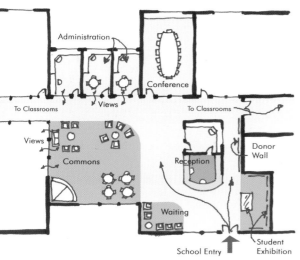

The placement of the reception area in this conceptual plan allows for the easy greeting and directing of visitors as they enter the school. Its surrounding elements – waiting area, gallery for display of student work, and donor wall – reflect the values of care, personalization, academic rigor, and stewardship.

their own ways to contribute to a place that values permeability, nurture, growth, and development. The importance of a good first impression also plays out in schools. Expectation, tone, and attitude become readily apparent as one observes teacher interactions with other adults and with students, students' regard for the school, and the standards and expectations of the entire school community.

▶ **IN PRACTICE**

Make sure their first steps into your small school invite people into a place of safety, warmth, and involvement. The design of your entrance area can help students, parents, staff, and community members feel greeted and connected to the mutual teaching and learning that takes place here.

3. Wayfinding and Streetscapes

This child development center utilizes varied animal symbols to guide learners to their grade-appropriate learning spaces.

Once inside a small school, no one should get lost, either literally or figuratively. Its building design achieves this goal when it provides elements that invite people to "read" where they stand, where they are going, and what they might pass along the way. As people make their way along the corridors in a small school, they should feel as they do walking down a lively, peopled street. Full of interest and event, passageways bring people together and lead them toward new learning at every step.

Like a city, a building uses landmarks, nodes, districts, and paths to help people situate themselves and others as they use it. Can students easily orient themselves and find their way around the school? Can visitors easily find their way to the media lab from the reception area?

Floor patterns, colors, lighting, or textures can serve a wayfinding function as people move through a building. At one school that overlooks a salmon spawning stream, a symbolic stream with fish embedded in the floor pattern meanders through the interior and links it to the outdoor courtyard and the stream beyond.

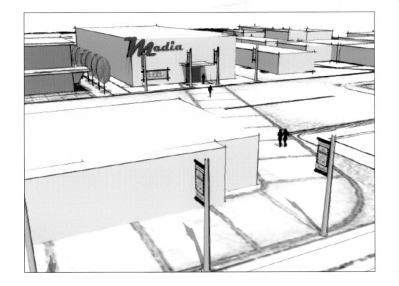

When a large, comprehensive high school transforms itself into multiple small learning environments, thoughtfully placed signage helps to reorient people to the building's new organization.

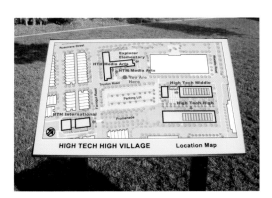

A village of six small schools places directional maps throughout its property to orient visitors.

Wayfinding elements become particularly crucial when adults and students must re-orient themselves to new small learning communities on a campus they may have navigated for years. Campus maps – color-coded by small learning community – at strategic locations throughout the school provide visual clues to the new uses of space. Signage, in prominent positions at key entry points and along central campus organizers, can also signal a small school's or learning community's boundaries. Painting lines on concrete walkways, in different colors that signify different learning communities or small schools, helps replace old circulation patterns with fresh ones designed to build autonomy.

Hallways and corridors, in addition to providing a useful ribbon of connection among the different areas of a school, may serve to break down the scale of a larger building, making it feel familiar and accessible. The traditional high school hallway crops up regularly in movies and nightmares as a bleak

Adding some "wiggle to the walk" of the conventional straight-line school corridor creates opportunities for the development of dynamic interior streetscapes. The exhibition of student work, vistas into classrooms, and nodes for informal meeting and gathering introduce additional elements of variety and surprise.

and lonely labyrinth of exposure and humiliation. But in a good small school or small learning community within a larger school, a hallway can provide a warm and social thoroughfare, giving those who travel it a look at the people, the work, and the ideas that surround them.

Just as in the streets of a city, people meet in a school's halls, and they often want a place to stop and talk. While remaining aware of entrance and egress requirements, adding "a wiggle in the walk" by designing a few niches set into the length of a corridor will prompt people to linger for a few moments without getting in the way of others. In a multiplex, as students remain in their small learning community, hallways can increasingly become collaborative and learning-centered spaces, as opposed to busy highways.

Convention frowns on such hallway socializing, and indeed, most schools work hard to clear their corridors of loiterers. At the same time they invite noise and congestion by locating lockers in hallways, which also limits the wall area available for student work or views into classrooms.

Far from serving merely as a means to get the crowd from one point to another, the hallway should create a rich and complex indoor landscape of learning and opportunity. Its walls function as galleries displaying student

In addition to moving students from one space to another, this hallway invites learners to acknowledge the accomplishments of their peers, discuss new ideas, participate in impromptu tutoring sessions, and take a break from a busy day.

art or other works; at its nodes people stop to refresh themselves with food or drink; and it provides seating where people might pause to exchange ideas or information. Not least for adolescents, the hallway functions in the time-honored tradition of the paseo, a meandering passage meant for displaying oneself and regarding others.

Essential arteries that carry the lifeblood of a school, hallways should also lead us past windows and entranceways from which we can see students and teachers at work. Whatever role we take in the school community, the corridors should tempt us and provoke our thought, stir our imagination and inspire us to new endeavor.

▶ **IN PRACTICE**

Allow the people who walk through your small high school to see far enough that they know where they stand. Provide visual elements to help them find their way through the space. Transform the halls of your small school into passages filled with opportunities to see and participate in the varied work of the learning community. Display, conversation, and observation should all play a part in a hallway's streetscape.

4. *Distributed Resources*

A School for the Entrepreneur
B Bio-Med Academy
C Global Connections
D International School of Communications
E Community Commons

(N) SITE PLAN

The four three-story small schools on this educational campus each contain administrative and counseling offices, teacher workrooms, and student common areas. A centrally located "community commons" houses a variety of campus-wide amenities including a gymnasium, kitchen, large dining area, and nurse's office.

Students in a small school should have easy access to its student services and academic resources. Services such as cafeterias, administrative offices, and health clinics, as well as learning resources like project rooms, specialty labs, and libraries, all exist to help students thrive in school. Their placement should create a sense of promise, welcome, trust, and community.

Small schools face important choices and challenges as they decide where to place the resources and services they want to make accessible to all students. For example, clustering food services and the library in a central area can create a "town square" where one goes to do business and mingle with others in the community. On the other hand, dispersing small guidance offices and administrators to different points in the school can lend a more personal, family-like tone and counter what might otherwise seem like a centralized, adult-oriented bureaucracy.

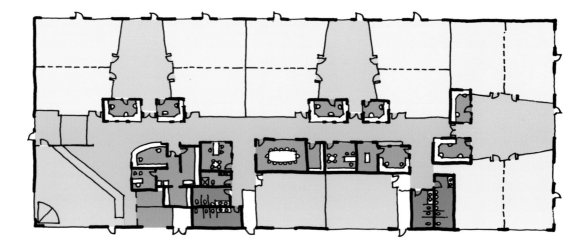

Whole school learning spaces

Office and administrative spaces

Specialty labs

Bathrooms

Classrooms

Rather than locating all administrative functions together in an office wing or building, small offices can be placed at the entrance of each learning cluster. Such placement allows for more efficient student access to supportive adults.

Clustering staff in professional workspaces encourages collaboration, but distributing such offices in smaller units helps connect staff with students.

A small school's central goal is to remain firmly student-centered; remembering this can sometimes help resolve sticky issues of where to locate administrative staff. When every adult in a school has regular and meaningful contact with students, the school is fulfilling its mission, and placement of its resources will follow logically.

Large schools in the process of dividing into smaller learning communities sometimes have a tendency to resist decentralizing the areas that they have long consolidated into administrative offices. In some cases, they agree on a gradual process of converting the space to better meet the needs of the

In order to be closer to the small learning community with which she worked, this high school administrator converted an underutilized janitorial closet into a gracious office space.

whole building. As each small school's administrative team relocates closer to its own classrooms and staff, what was once the main office can become central space for professional development, a health clinic, a parent center, and/or a place of initial entry where visitors are greeted and directed to the various small schools on a campus.

Smaller restrooms and cafes distributed throughout the school might feel more inviting and safe than large ones that serve more people at once. Even if a large kitchen prepares the food, some schools warm and serve it in separate eating areas in each small learning community. In warmer climates, many schools arrange for food-vending carts in outdoor gathering spaces where students relax and eat at tables or benches. Maintenance functions can also be distributed in the small school community. When students help keep classrooms, common areas, and restrooms neat and clean, a strong sense develops of shared responsibility for their school environment.

When members of a small school or small learning community dine together, a sense of community grows. Here, an intimate eating area has been established.

Rather than building a central library, this small school created "library nooks" throughout the campus. Students gain easy access to resource materials and inviting environments in which to read and research.

Small school environments where students are well known, where the sense of safety is high, and where ownership and a community culture prevail encourage freedom of movement and access to a variety of resources. It strengthens the fabric of a school when students can come and go to project areas, leaving work in progress out; when they can conduct research in outdoor learning spaces; and when they can find technology-enabled workstations wherever and whenever they need them.

▷ **IN PRACTICE**

Place resources and services that affect students within their easy reach. Arrange for all adults on your small school's staff to have regular contact with students, and make it natural for them to encounter each other on their daily rounds.

5. Safety

The small high school derives its greatest security from mutual knowledge, trust, respect, and communication among the members of its community. Any design elements that foster those characteristics will contribute as much to the safety of its occupants as would the most elaborate security measures available.

In recent years, many large high schools have turned into fortified bulwarks, defending against the incursions of undesirable people and objects. Metal detectors guard their entrances; video cameras monitor their stairwells; chain-link fences with padlocked gates surround their asphalt lots; security officers patrol their corridors. A sense of mutual low-level hostility and dread suffuses the interactions between students and adults. The consequences of a young person's antisocial behavior escalate from detention to expulsion, and the focus on compliance and control rather than respect and responsibility only contributes to an unsafe environment. Such settings appear to be preparing students for prison rather than for productivity in college, work, and citizenship. Against this bleak backdrop, small high schools are trying

At left: Clear visibility into a school's various spaces functions as passive security. When adults can easily view student gathering areas from their offices or classrooms, they provide unintrusive "eyes on the street."

anew to instill civility, respect, permeability, and safety into the places where adolescents learn.

The sense that "everyone knows everyone" in a small school can have a profound effect on the security of the community. People notice, for example, when a stranger enters the building or when someone behaves in an inappropriate way. And if small schools work hard to build a culture of communication, collaboration, and trust, typically someone speaks up about such things in time to avert a threat to the community's welfare.

A school's building design can also amplify and enhance the factors that lead to a secure environment. It can include a formal reception area where someone greets people who enter, signs them in, and directs them to the appropriate places. Using interior windows and strategic sightlines, a school's design can create common areas and work spaces that lie clearly in other people's view, providing opportunities for additional "eyes on the street" that offer additional security. Dispersing adults throughout the building makes the places where they work easily accessible to students seeking safe haven.

Developing a culture of respect and responsibility on a large campus converted into small learning communities is an evolutionary process. Initially, passive security may not be sufficient if a preexisting culture of anonymity and distrust prevails. However, as small school identity and ownership increase,

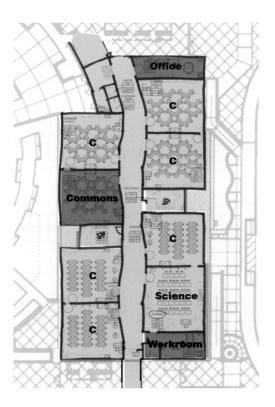

traditional forms of security will become less imperative. Providing contiguous space for each small learning community, coupled with the strategic positioning of administrative offices at small-school entrance points, should quickly establish a safer environment. For instance, a small learning community located on one floor of a larger building might "bookend" the hall with administrative offices at one end and teacher collaborative areas at the other.

Outside the building, thoughtful design can provide adequate lighting for parking and pathways and keep shrubbery low so people can see each other. And it can provide welcoming spaces in which small groups of students and their adult advisers can come to know each other well and observe each other's work, developing the norms of trust and respect that will guide their behavior.

Designers must stay sensitive to the school's context. A rural community where people do not even lock the doors to their homes has different security needs than an urban environment where surveillance cameras and emergency

Well-lit outdoor public spaces and pathways, extensive use of windows, and appropriate use of vegetation contribute to a sense of security and enhance everyone's ability to see and be seen.

phones may be required until a more personalized school culture matures. In any context, however, designers can contribute to a safe environment by creating a place where people readily notice each other's comings and goings. A more transparent school can feel at once warmer, more open, and more secure, if it matches its precautions with a spirit of genuine interest in each person's welfare.

▶ **IN PRACTICE**

Treat safety and security as a human issue, not merely a mechanical one. Design your school to maximize the degree to which people see, know, and communicate with one another. Provide security mechanisms that will operate in people's absence and invest equally in resources that will build trust within the community.

6. Lifelong Fitness

Unlike traditional high school gym classes that focus on competitive sports, this fitness center helps students develop healthy habits for life.

Just as a school's design invites thoughtful intellectual discourse, so it can offer students opportunities to develop the lifelong habits that will keep them in good physical health. Indoors and outdoors, a good small high school has enough choices for maintaining fitness that students of all different types can stay active and learn new ways to keep well.

Too often, high school gym classes have focused solely on competitive sports, favoring students with athletic prowess at the expense of those less coordinated. But physical education in small high schools is turning in new directions, matching the ways their academics focus on the individual needs of students. Research has shown that learning benefits come with plenty of exercise, and these schools are aiming to ensure that every student graduates with habits of fitness that will last a lifetime.

Lifelong fitness involves paying attention to the interests and capacities of individual students and also creating fitness facilities that can adapt to a variety of activities. Wherever they go in the school buildings and grounds, people should find some means to let off steam in physical activity – on their own, and in small or large groups.

Resources outside the school can be leveraged for physical fitness. Nearby gyms, pools, health clubs, parks, and playing fields can provide opportunities for exercise.

Many schools provide a gymnasium in which to play indoor games that require plenty of room and a floor designed for athletic use. Playing fields, too, best support certain popular outdoor sports. But small schools whose location precludes these possibilities have found access to such facilities in a shared building, a commercial fitness center, or a neighborhood park. They have also embedded into their own locations various smaller-scale opportunities for fitness.

A large exterior or interior wall, for example, could turn into a place to learn rock-climbing with only a modest investment of equipment. By clearing a small room of furniture, adding carpeting or a few mats, and insuring proper ventilation, one might create a yoga and exercise studio. A few stationary bicycles in a corner of a common space could encourage aerobic activities as a way of socializing.

The installation of a climbing wall transforms a standard gymnasium into a space that also welcomes more personal challenges.

Outdoor fitness does not require complicated equipment to be effective. One can carry out a full body circuit of exercise by running up a hill and stopping to stretch at boulders, park benches, steps, trees, even parking meters.

Alongside outdoor paths, a school can install the simple apparatus – like chin-up bars or low hurdles – that turn it into a fitness trail. Basketball hoops at strategic locations can get kids playing pickup games in their spare minutes.

With a few pieces of equipment and adequate ventilation, regular classrooms can be transformed into workout studios.

Wellness can be integrated into a small learning community's curriculum focus; a health sciences academy, for example, may include nutrition and physical therapy coursework. Some schools offer wellness classes in which students devise individual fitness plans tailored to their needs and goals and carry them out on their own. The teacher serves as coach and adviser, taking fitness readings at regular intervals. By encouraging kinesthetic awareness along with healthy choices, such activities prepare students for later life when their level of fitness will be their own daily decision.

▶ **IN PRACTICE**

Take advantage of any indoor or outdoor space that could invite physical activity, either on a small or a larger scale. Equip it in ways that suit individuals as well as groups.

Learning-Focused

*Learning is active and based on the interests
and ability of each individual.
The facility supports the discovery
of what each child can know and do,
harnesses the resources of the school and
community, and respectfully expects
much of each student and adult.*

The entry to this Native American school serves as a community gathering and performance space, showcases cultural artifacts, and references an adjacent river.

At left: When utilizing this small school's commons space, students are surrounded by the school's core values.

Those who approach or enter a small school will immediately experience a strong impression of its identity if they encounter a symbolic "signature." The building itself can function as that symbol, as can features such as signs, artwork, installations, and materials that convey the central identity of the institution and "the way we learn around here." Yet "learning" should be the most powerful signature for a school. Emphasizing its importance can influence everything in the school – space, architectural details, furnishings, colors, and graphics.

The classic architecture of comprehensive high schools constructed during the late nineteenth and early twentieth centuries reflects the reverence with which the American population of that era regarded public education. Imposing solid brick and stone buildings manifested civic pride and a belief in the importance and permanence of learning at a time when vast numbers of immigrants and working-class Americans went to school to gain a better life.

Those structures also stood as symbols of that era's philosophy of education. Primary and secondary schools, like the factories of the industrial age,

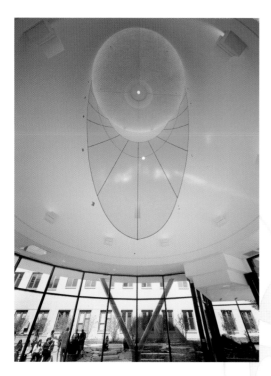

This school's centrally located sundial pays tribute to Mexican culture and commemorates the nineteen-day hunger strike that preceded the building's construction.

efficiently sorted students into a level of instruction matched with their social class and gender. Students regularly learned by rote, in neat rows of desks that faced a lecturer, preparing for jobs they often kept for the rest of their lives. School served as an agent for assimilation into the dominant culture, as an immigrant population took on a new American identity.

Now, in the twenty-first century, small public high schools are celebrating diversity rather than assimilation, seeking to create equity rather than sorting learners. Instead of selecting certain students to succeed, they aim to prepare students for a society that requires higher-order thinking skills of everyone. By tailoring curriculum to fit students' needs, interests, and learning styles, they hope to see all children achieve at high levels.

Autonomous small schools are proliferating, springing up across the country. Architecture can help with this identity building as long as a robust school philosophy of learning underlies its designs.

This new philosophy reflects changing realities and aspirations, and school architecture calls on new symbols to convey them. For example, a new educational complex of small high schools in a predominantly Latino neighborhood won funding from a public school district only after parents staged a nineteen-day hunger strike. In honor of their passion and victory, a sundial

This mural, which calls out courage, discipline, and perseverance, captures the small school's focus on preparing all of its inner-city students for college and beyond.

in the school's central courtyard now marks the passage of time through every day of learning.

Exterior and interior details of color and texture, materials and finishes, ornamentation and display objects can all perform this symbolic function. They can make a school stand out from any other, manifest its individual identity, and evoke a distinct tone that has everything to do with the ethos of the school. Students at a small school with an emphasis on high technology can see the bundled cables of its computer infrastructure overhead, evoking the school's signature as a place of "work made visible." Read-only displays of key school data, such as temperature and energy use, can transform the physical classroom into a teaching tool.

The entry halls of many high schools display murals painted by students, vivid symbols evoking the school's community of learners. In one school, each new student and teacher creates a computer-generated image mounted on an acrylic tile to reflect a unique identity that is added to a wall mosaic that grows larger every year. A prominent banner or slogan can have a similar cohesive effect; one small high school displays its yearly "essential question"

The hub of this high school's ninth grade academy – a small house – communicates personalization and community to all academy members.

on a banner in the entryway, inviting everyone to join in the inquiry that unifies the curriculum across the school.

As suburbs mushroomed with sprawl and sameness in recent decades, their ever-larger high schools relied on a standard organization and curriculum that differed little from place to place. But in this new era, a growing number of suburban schools are choosing to break into smaller learning communities, each with its individual stamp.

A bold entry helps this small high school distinguish itself from the two other small schools that share the campus, once a large, comprehensive high school.

On a large campus, each small learning community's identity should be clear to all who enter and travel through its space. In some cases, this identity is shaped by the building or area of campus that houses it. A ninth-grade academy in Los Angeles designed its space around a house-like structure with shutters and a fireplace, and those who inhabit it describe the academy as a warm, intimate family. Symbolic logos on doorways and at the entrance to the community, as well as colors chosen for each learning community, help give each group a signature with which to define itself and build on design elements used by the central campus. Such "branding" helps to distinguish the individual school's community from those that surround it. At the same time, a school's true signature develops and deepens with time, as each small learning community becomes more focused, coherent, and distinct.

▶ **IN PRACTICE**

Pay attention to the central philosophy of the school and seek to understand how it relates to the particular community it serves. Then arrange symbols, spaces, and furnishings that evoke that learning philosophy and position them so as to express the school's unique identity to all who approach.

8. Display

Display of student work at this small school is paramount. At every turn, student work makes standards visible, continually raising the bar for good work.

Small high schools rest their reputations on the quality of student work, displaying it both formally and informally throughout their buildings. By doing so, they continually raise the bar for good work as students take a look at what others do and try to match or better it.

In a large and anonymous high school, the report card functions as the indicator of how students are doing. A private document, it labels achievement by letter or number, making it almost impossible to imagine the human effort, thought, skill, creativity, or individuality that contributed to the grades a student receives.

This dry and soulless record of assessment stands in stark opposition to the celebration of good work that meets the eye continually when one enters a good small high school. Its entryways, halls, classrooms, and commons areas show off student work on walls, shelves, pedestals, and other display structures. Whether the work consists of visual art or poetry, robotic inventions or scale models, it provides concrete evidence of student learning to a com-

A prominently displayed student-created glider illustrates a real-world application of the physics principles explored in this classroom lab.

munity hungry for accountability. Just as important, it fills the school with a contagious sense of accomplishment and pride in tasks well done.

Any work that goes on display merits a high level of professionalism in its presentation. Alongside artwork and photographs, for example, students might provide short artist's statements explaining their materials and rationale. Similarly, charts and written materials might have an accompanying title, central question, or text that explains their purpose to the viewer. Everything the school displays represents its standards, so clarity, neatness, and mechanics of spelling and punctuation matter.

Easy access to display mechanisms encourages use and frequent updating of student work.

If galleries and display spaces are easily accessible for changing the work they hold, they will remain a fresh point of interest throughout the school year. Along the walls of a hallway one might build shallow picture rails on which portfolios or art can rest. Walls made of sturdy fiberboard panels could hold a movable feast of student products and their accompanying signs or explanatory notes. Framed photographs or artwork could hang by wires

Large high schools often have a variety of built-in display cases. Rather than housing photographs or trophies of graduates long gone, they can become perfect venues for spotlighting student accomplishments.

from a ledge near the ceiling. Large objects like gliders and human-powered submarines can be suspended from the ceiling, and lobby areas can project video projects on flat-screen televisions. One school fashioned an ingenious hallway display system of floor-to-ceiling metal rods with clamps for mounting work at various levels.

Plexiglas display cabinets provide protected areas for three-dimensional objects. Many large high schools use such cabinets to display trophies and photographs from graduates long gone, but they can be reclaimed by small learning communities for student work. Locker space may be at a premium, but some schools remove portions of locker bays in key locations, then build recessed display cabinets within the wall openings, to showcase student work.

When common spaces are disconnected from a community of learners – the norm in comprehensive high schools – vandalism commonly occurs, and so adults may avoid displaying student work. However, as small school identity and culture build in conversion high schools, respect for student work also increases among students. In the interim, the installation of high

This dedicated art gallery facilitates the ongoing showcasing of artistic as well as academic student accomplishments.

tack rails can facilitate display, keeping showcased projects out of easy reach.

Schools with a strong commitment to the arts or engineering sometimes dedicate a separate gallery space to student work. But wherever they choose to display what students know and do, small schools make a statement about the value they place on their students' accomplishments by presenting them to the community.

▶ **IN PRACTICE**

Use every opportunity to build in display spaces that can bring attention to student work of all types, shapes, and sizes. Provide easy access to display mechanisms so that new work can regularly take the place of old.

Though not directly involved in one another's work, these two learners – given the transparent environment – can appreciate and benefit from the other's diligence.

At left: This visible multipurpose lab, currently used for robotics, allows students to see one another engaged in interesting work and to learn from the exposed mechanical systems overhead.

People ought to witness learning as it happens in a good small school. Learning is contagious; success is seductive. Seeing other students engaged in interesting work can make young people want to do it too. When anyone in the school community can observe students at work, high standards become everyone's business, and then expectations carry more weight. Students feel more welcome to approach teachers if the school's design makes access to adult workspaces easy and visible. The school becomes a safer place as well when most of the actions within it have a public aspect.

Professional workplaces commonly create environments in which the work takes place in full view. Newsrooms hum with activity and energy as the clock ticks toward the deadline. Software developers and architects work out their ideas together, drawing on each other's creativity. These people aren't just collaborating; they are learning from each other, taking away new information and strategies that will help them provide better solutions to future problems. Transparency like this can also raise standards. Out of the corner of the eye, people notice what peers are doing and adjust their own work to match. If a school values active learning on the part of students, it helps to offer them a look at what others are working on.

Students feel welcome to approach teachers if the school's design makes access to adults' work spaces easy and visible. When adult work areas are adjacent to high-traffic student areas, teachers and administrators stay more tuned in to what's happening there.

But most high schools still close the doors on the work of students and teachers. Too often they herd people into drab and isolated boxes, feed them predigested information for use on standardized tests, and then lament that nobody has much appetite for teaching or learning. Despite their crowding, most high schools like this are lonely places for both young people and adults.

At first, teachers may worry whether students will pay attention to their work if interior windows reveal their classrooms to others in the school. This is particularly true in large comprehensive high schools with long-standing cultures of teaching and learning in isolation. But when teachers try it, they often find that everybody seems to be invigorated by what's happening around them. In today's information age, many teenagers are used to multitasking and a visually stimulating environment; having others within view does not seem to bother them. For many, it may actually reflect the vibrant activity level of their home lives, making school a more comfortable setting in which to learn.

The circulation corridors in some small schools are designed as internal streets. Storefront windows offer views into classrooms, teachers' offices, and administrative spaces. The life and learning of the school community is clearly and consistently on display. The understated "omnipresence" of adults provides passive supervision and helps create a culture in which students can feel safe as they move about freely throughout the building.

An open door policy can create transparency into classrooms such as this, where a small window inhibits meaningful visibility.

Seeing into laboratory spaces and studios invites students' interest in trying new things from robotic inventions to biology dissections or historical role-plays. Teachers become accustomed to sharing what they're trying in the curriculum and inviting feedback when they get used to others occasionally looking in on them.

Older high school buildings typically lack interior windows, which makes transparent teaching and learning challenging for the small learning communities housed within them. Small, rectangular door windows represent the only views into classrooms and typically, in an effort to focus student attention, teachers cover them. At a minimum, small learning communities should require such windows to remain clear. Some even adopt an open door policy. As the small school culture of rigorous learning increases and student distractibility decreases, resources may be directed toward

A transparent conference room invites students, faculty, and visitors to witness student-student, student-staff, and school-community collaboration.

providing doors with larger expanses of glass and/or windows from hallways into classrooms.

A more transparent school environment also affects the emotional tone of a school. As teachers observe students in contexts outside their own classroom, they may see strengths they can use to address academic challenges. Socially as well as academically, adults also provide a visible model for students to learn from.

When they readily can see adults around, kids get the sense that they can approach them for help. This has academic significance, increasing the personal character of the learning environment. But just as important, the school grows safer and more secure when interpersonal encounters take place largely within others' view. If a conversation ought to remain confidential, the blinds can always go down in a windowed office.

Visitors from the outside community feel much more welcome and informed in a school where they can witness students at work without intruding into

* Key for prospective students + families

classroom space. This has a double benefit. First, it encourages the public to contribute to the school, whether by their participation and expertise or by actual money or materials. Second, it includes the members of the community in maintaining high standards and expectations as they see and critique the work their (taxes support.)

tuition / donor dollars

Not such a good argument

Obviously, not every space in a school should remain open to view. Theatrical performance spaces, for example, require carefully controlled lighting, as do photographic darkrooms. But when a school takes on the habit of exhibiting its learning, visibility in its building design can follow more often than not.

▶ **IN PRACTICE**

Always ask how a space might allow others to witness the learning that takes place there from both within the space and outside it. If possible, open up that view in an inviting way while still suiting its proportions and acoustics to the needs of the learners.

The work areas in a school mirror the variety of activities its learning community embraces. If people are asked to collaborate, the school needs to provide formal and informal spaces in which to meet; if they work independently or require peaceful spaces to retreat, they need areas made for that, too. Lectures, experiments, the building of models, and the making of art all require different kinds of space. At best, a small school's design includes a variety of spaces that easily adapt to serve different functions.

In everything they do, teenagers are working to define their individual identities, the chief developmental task of adolescence. Yet high school provides few spaces for them to come together in the personal exchanges with adults and with peers in which they can build trust and take some tentative steps on the path to self-definition. Instead, schools tend to herd kids into larger groups, concentrating on controlling their behavior rather than developing it.

Merely forming a smaller learning community does not go far enough to create a culture in which students are known well. Nor does it help much for a large school to supply a menu of clubs and activities in which kids

At left: The attention a small school gives to individual students manifests itself in areas where they can pursue independent learning, reflecting their interests and talents.

can get together. Students need a dependable academic setting that supports connection, reflection, mentoring, advising, and other interactions in which adults and other students come to know them well. This personalization helps them prepare for success in college, work, and civic life.

Young people and adults should have plenty of informal opportunities to meet and linger in conversation.

Schools encourage formal and informal interactions when they incorporate alcoves conducive to conversation into hallways, classrooms, and other areas that usually hold larger groups of students. Certain places naturally appeal as informal gathering spots where accidental encounters and spontaneous interactions can occur. Courtyard edges and outdoor setting areas seem to draw people, whatever the climate. Crossroads or nodes where people make a choice to turn in one direction or another are equally compelling. A window-seat, a picnic table, a couch, or a group of comfortable chairs in a common area invite students to stop and interact with peers and teachers. Some schools place seminar rooms, tutoring stations, carrels, or work stations at strategic locations, intended for use by those who are collaborating on work.

Entry signage, vegetation, color elements, and an amphitheater gathering space lend personality to this otherwise nondescript bungalow area.

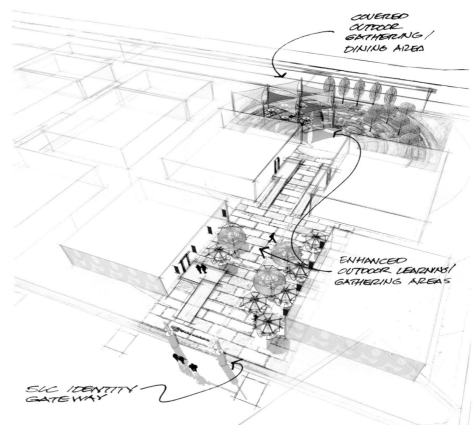

Small conference rooms, rather than being reserved for adult conversation, can provide ideal locations for Socratic seminars, small-group dialogue, student exhibitions, and advisories.

While at first glance creating such small group gathering spaces in already overcrowded school buildings may seem untenable, most existing high school campuses do have a variety of unused or underutilized storage, office, and conference areas. Reclaiming these spaces can allow them to be reused for more student-centered purposes.

The attention a small school gives to individual students also manifests itself in areas where they can pursue independent learning. Library-style carrels send this message, as do workstations clustered in suites of three or four. Valuing each student's progress involves personal coaching which requires space, too. In one school, tutors meet with students in a row of diner-style booths with high tops, affording privacy along with a comfortable, personal tone. That same school has adapted a series of inactive elevator shafts in the center of the building to serve as small tutoring rooms.

Schools whose curriculum encourages projects need the kind of work areas where students can function productively in the untidy ways that hands-on learning often involves. They may need room to spread materials out on large tables or to work with liquids or paints without worrying about damaging surfaces or floors. They may need adaptable walls or electrical systems and places to display projects or safely store work in progress. When high schools convert into small learning communities, many discover that underutilized or abandoned shop areas provide ideal spaces for such project-based learning.

Equally important, people should be able to find places protected from the fray throughout the school. Even a small room, if it has a door that shuts and a comfortable place to sit, provides a sense of sheltered, cave-like comfort. Position alone may set an area apart as a place of refuge. A perch above the crowd, perhaps on a staircase, can grant a few moments of calm when someone feels besieged. A cubby-like computer workstation might feel like a place one can escape. One school designated a room on each corner of its building as the "quiet room" or conference room, free from normal clatter

Some small schools provide individual workstations for students. These autonomous spaces give students a sense of ownership and are used as mini-studios for individual and collaborative work, storage for projects and supplies, and personal display of individuality.

Strategically placed groupings of comfortable seating provide students with places to connect, regroup, and retreat.

and chatter. And within larger or more public areas like libraries, hallways, classrooms, or music and art studios, one can create small alcoves with comfortable seating, which offer relative solitude and peace.

▶ **IN PRACTICE**

For every space designed for a large group, give equal thought to providing for those who will learn best in a smaller one. Create small private areas throughout your building for independent work and for small groups to gather in productive study and conversation. Wherever people would naturally stop to talk in your school, design a place to make them welcome. Punctuate your small school with spaces to which a person can retreat for peace and quiet reflection.

II. *Studios and Specialty Labs*

This small school's flexible "great room" accommodates all-school meetings, small-group tutoring, and a variety of exploratory, hands-on learning activities, including a rock band.

At left: Small high schools substitute depth for breadth with a few important learning priorities that allow students to go deeply into a particular field of interest. The learning habits and skills they acquire will serve them well when they approach other subjects.

High school students do some of their most powerful learning in places that do not look at all like classrooms. Hands-on projects, experiments, creative expression, and other experiences that involve the body as much as the mind require a particular kind of studio or laboratory setting. Applied learning spaces designed for maximum flexibility and adaptability contribute to a small school that equally stretches the capacities of all students.

The traditional high school built science laboratories and vocational or technical shops to serve a curriculum that firmly separated future white-collar workers from those who would enter the trades. Specialty teachers presided over the wood shop or metal shop, the chemistry lab or the art room, guarding their domains and routing students to their destined futures. One of the arguments for the large comprehensive high school was that it offered the full array of such specialty areas; students could pick and choose as in a shopping mall whose shelves hold everything one can imagine.

Small high schools typically set aside that breadth, choosing instead to go deeper into a few important learning experiences. If teachers know students well enough, the reasoning goes, they can coach them to try new challenges that grow from their individual interests, goals, and needs. All students can perform at a high level, these schools hold, and they will all achieve if the school helps them use their hands along with their minds to address fundamental questions in every field of learning.

Following this vision, however, requires special work areas in which students can explore all kinds of hands-on learning. Instead of a chemistry lab, for example, a school might design a laboratory that could adapt to a variety of scientific explorations. Its floor and furnishings, impervious to the wet and smelly effects of experimentation, would suit any number of projects, and its technical aspects – electrical systems, plumbing, sound, ventilation, computer infrastructure – would also anticipate their demands. Such a multipurpose laboratory would depend on well-designed storage for discipline-specific materials and equipment, but it could pay off in making high-quality space available for every class involving active scientific investigation.

Likewise, a school could build a project area intended to accommodate students who build things, invent or design things, and make art. Some schools with embedded small learning communities create large and open shop areas (or "toolboxes") with glass partitions that separate noisy and

Rather than designing course-specific science labs, this small school in New York City opted for multipurpose labs, capable of accommo- dating all levels of science as well as a variety of other project-based learning activities.

Learning clusters in this small school are organized around multipurpose studios that accommodate a wide-range of hands-on learning activities.

dirty activities while lending an overall sense of people working with their hands. At various stations students might be using a saw or a drill press, creating a clay sculpture, designing a robot, or building an electric guitar. These spaces, when surrounded by academic class-rooms, can emphasize the best of academic pedagogy (its rigor-ous content) and the best of vocational pedagogy (its hands-on methodology).

Some small schools with a very specific thematic focus (such as music and dance, firefighting, or engineering) require highly technical studio or lab spaces that go beyond multipurpose classrooms. Here again, the philosophy "less is more" explains the compromise they make by choosing one field instead of many. As students go deeply into a particular field of interest, they are learning habits and skills that will serve them well when they approach other subjects in later life or education. A school based on aviation would ideally be located at an airfield, with access to a hangar and other specialty resources. An arts academy could have its own gallery along with photography and dance studios.

This former shop classroom is now used by a small learning community on campus for media technology applications.

Even a school with only traditional classrooms available can incorporate project studios into its building design. One high school offers an American studies course in which a teaching team works with a large group of students in adjoining classrooms. One room serves as a quieter space for lectures, discussion, and research; in the other, students work on constructing projects, making art, and other hands-on activities.

Because such labs and project studios reflect the small school's philosophy of personalized, project-based learning, sharing those spaces with a larger school poses a thorny dilemma. Small learning communities that occupy a larger building might consider keeping their science and hands-on learning areas as separate as any other classroom, preserving their autonomy and individualism as a crucial element of school culture.

In older buildings, relocating science classrooms can be costly and complicated, but economical alternatives exist. Some science courses merely require classrooms with sinks and appropriate storage; or, if necessary, a school can purchase portable fume hoods, eyewash stations, and sinks. Small schools

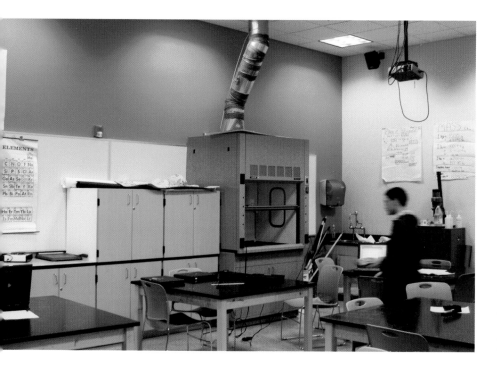

Chemsurf tabletops, portable Bunsen burners, a sink, and a chemistry hood are all that were needed to transform this general classroom into a science-ready learning environment.

under one roof might also adopt the shared-space model that colleges often use in science courses: Day-to-day instruction occurs in multi-purpose labs (staffed by a para-educator with a science background, or even a lab technician from a partner institution), and teachers sign up as necessary for other labs equipped for high-end investigations.

Such sharing of space and resources allows most science instruction to occur within small learning communities and facilitates teacher collaboration and interdisciplinary instruction. When several small learning communities must use science classrooms grouped in a single building, assigning rooms and demarcating them with small school logos and colors builds ownership and protects small school autonomy.

▷ **IN PRACTICE**

In designing work areas for students, put applied learning and hands-on activities on an equal footing with more abstract intellectual pursuits. Build project studios and laboratories with maximum flexibility so they can adapt to a variety of individual needs for experimentation and expression.

12. Presentation

In part, small learning communities hold themselves accountable to high standards by routinely asking students to present their work before an audience. Whether that involves a classroom project or an on-stage concert, streaming video or a virtual field trip, the physical context should support and contribute to student exhibition. Lighting, acoustics, wiring, room size, and staging all affect the quality of a presentation.

Authentic assessment often requires students to present their work to adult audiences. Small schools need formal and informal venues for such presentation – venues with adequate light, open spaces, large presentation surfaces, and furniture that can be easily reconfigured.

The conventional high school relies on paper-and-pencil tests as its primary means for assessing what students know and can do. But most small high schools prefer to have students demonstrate their understanding of a topic by also presenting their knowledge, ideas, or skills and undergoing the scrutiny and questions of a critical audience. Such exhibitions and presentations generally demand more of students, foster their authentic work and mastery, and let them show what they know outside the narrow scope of a testmaker's questions.

This commons space includes a variety of deliberate design choices – retractable curtain, sloped seating, platform stage, circular layout, acoustic panels, projection unit, and sound system – that allow it to accommodate varied types of student presentation.

Schools have long provided performance space for the arts in which to present concerts, drama, and dance. Yet student presentations arising from academic contexts also frequently need to take place on stage. Students from a literature class, for example, might act out scenes from a book they are reading; a social studies class might role-play a trial or a historical debate.

The traditional proscenium stage of a large high school auditorium often does not suit the needs of such smaller performances – and it can also cost a school dearly. Many schools have turned to smaller, more flexible performance spaces: black-box theaters, small performance studios, shoebox theaters, or curtained-off partitions with movable platforms that can be stacked for

A classroom with multi-use, movable furniture easily transforms into a stage for student performance.

seating or a stage. One school uses its grand staircase as a presentation space, with the audience on the stairs and the presenter on the landing. When climate permits, outdoor space such as a small amphitheater, or even a run of stairs, can also work well if its acoustics allow sound to carry.

Student performances and exhibitions greatly benefit when one builds the technological elements of a presentation space into classrooms and studios – an image projection and sound system, adequate electrical wiring and plugs, versatile lighting and room-darkening equipment. Movable walls or partitions allow classrooms or breakout spaces to convert swiftly into a larger presentation area. Commons areas, too, should have the capacity to stage a student presentation before a fair-sized audience with only minimal adaptation. Many multiplexes are building "great halls" for this purpose.

Design features like these contribute to a school culture in which students expect to show what they know before an audience. In the best small schools, students are performing at every turn, filling the place with vibrant evidence of their growth and learning.

▶ IN PRACTICE

Throughout your school, provide large and smaller spaces in which students may present and perform their work. Design regular classrooms and gathering areas to adapt to performance functions as well, and equip them with the technical elements that enhance both artistic and academic presentations.

13. Integrated Technology

This small school's library utilizes both desktop and laptop computers, which provide greater flexibility and encourage collaborative use.

In this digital age, high-tech tools at school should be as ubiquitous as pens and paper, so as to combine the best traditional learning approaches with the unprecedented opportunities technology offers. Wherever they are in a small school, students and teachers should have access to computers and other technological learning and communication tools for independent use or in small and large groups.

We used to point to the well-stocked high school computer lab, where classes would reserve time to develop skills and do research, as the cutting edge of educational technology. Computers were used in the same way as textbooks, with all students doing the same thing at the same time. But the explosive growth of the Internet, along with portable, easy-to-use multimedia technologies, has created exciting new opportunities for integrating technology and learning. These electronic resources allow us to customize learning, leveraging different learning approaches and providing new ways of accessing and manipulating information. Networked, wireless technologies have shifted time and space, making learning possible anywhere at any time.

Technology is integrated into the daily lives of these teachers and students, supporting and enhancing the school's academic program.

With this in mind, small schools should make networked computers available to teachers and students not just in classrooms, libraries, and computer labs, but in waiting areas, corridors, eating areas, and gyms, with wireless connections extending well beyond the walls of the school, when possible.

Pervasive computing sends a message about the norms of the school: If you want to know something, you can find it out; if you want to express yourself, you can do it. The focus then shifts from the computer to the work itself – and to the learner – as an active participant in a collaborative culture of inquiry.

In the classroom, computer technology can integrate seamlessly into teaching and learning. Direct instruction, brainstorming sessions, skills practice,

These students employ global positioning systems to map hallway coordinates as part of a mathematics project.

note-taking, research and investigation, mathematical modeling, writing, illustration, presentation, and many other classroom routines can benefit from the use of software applications, interactive whiteboards, or computer projection systems. Rather than one student at a computer struggling alone to master an application, several students might gather at a workstation to help each other as they collaborate on a task. Rolling carts with multiple laptop computers quickly convert a traditional classroom into a computer lab. Separate studios or laboratories might offer specialized technology for artistic or scientific exploration in fields like video or animation, engineering or molecular biology. Such specialty labs should be distributed amongst small learning communities on a campus as dictated by school themes and foci. At the same time, nomadic devices such as global positioning systems and personal digital assistants could free computer technology from its moorings in the building, making it possible for students to use laptops or small digital units for projects in the field or at home. Distance learning via the Internet can afford contact with students from other cultures and specialized or high-level instruction or mentorship to students at schools whose resources otherwise preclude it.

The small school's building design can do a great deal to support these new patterns of technology use. Its infrastructure, for example, must anticipate the pervasive presence of computer technology throughout the school, both with and without wiring. As curriculum and instruction change, computers

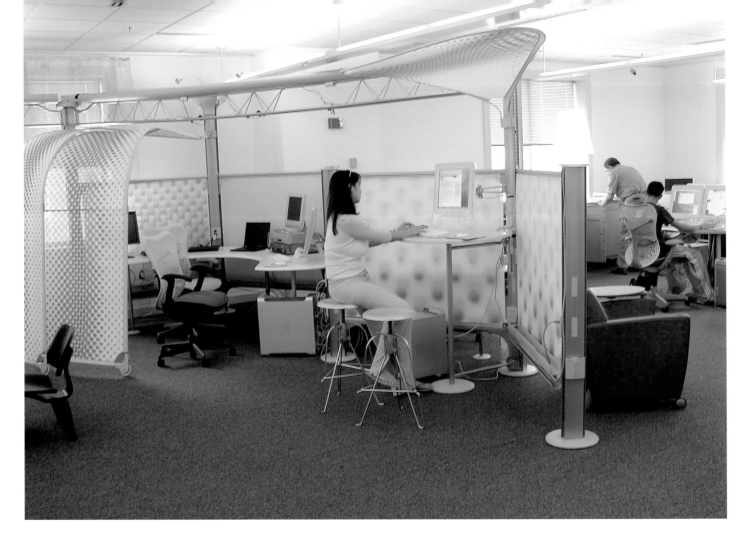

The building infrastructure must be flexible to support emerging technologies and tools. As curriculum and instruction change, computers and other electronic tools should be able to provide resources wherever they are needed.

will inevitably migrate from site to site in the school, and nothing in the school's wiring should inhibit this.

In addition to hardware and connectivity, digital content must include both curricular resources and productivity tools to support teaching approaches that meet a variety of learning preferences and needs. Schools must also plan ahead for continual professional development to keep teachers abreast of new technologies and applications; reliable technical support to keep everything running smoothly; and network backups to provide data redundancy.

A well-established culture of respect and responsibility allows this student to use portable technology away from immediate supervision.

A high school well equipped with technology faces special challenges. Despite all its potential for collaboration, computer use can be isolating, closing students off from their community as they are drawn into cyber-space. Also, computers (and especially portable devices) can tempt students to abscond with them, posing important security issues. Small schools have a powerful advantage in dealing with both these problems, because they work continually to build a culture of mutual trust between students and adults. When students feel known well and respected, and when they have confidence in at least one trusted adult in the school, they will take respon-sibility for each other and for the resources they share.

▶ **IN PRACTICE**

Treat information technology as a fundamental tool of learning, making it accessible everywhere in your small school and beyond. Foresee uses that go far beyond current resources and devices and build in the capacity to support them.

14. *Indoor and Outdoor Connections*

Garage-style doors represent an economical and practical way to blend indoor and outdoor learning environments. Such doors are common in shop spaces at comprehensive high schools.

At left: Where climate permits, benches, tables, and other amenities can expand the spaces of the school into the outdoors, providing new options for learning, meeting, and repose.

At their best, the indoor spaces of a small school connect and flow naturally into its outdoor spaces. People are drawn toward the light and landscape outside the rooms where they work, and for school people, the outdoors also presents opportunities for learning.

Why should we keep school indoors, closeting young people and their teachers away from the world? People in small schools tend to ask that question as they notice how students and adults gravitate toward the outdoors, for reasons that have just as much to do with learning as with purely social affairs.

For example, something attracts people to a sunny, clearly defined space just outside a building. A well-designed courtyard often forms the communal heart of a school, with students and adults seeking out its benches, sunlight, and shade to talk or relax. Similarly, people will gather in an inviting terrace at a school's entrance, a place connected to both the building and the land around it. Some small schools are incorporating both "front porch" and "back porch" elements into their designs. As with private homes, the front porch is more public, while the back porch is more protected and private.

Sprawling campuses often possess numerous outdoor gathering spaces. When large high schools convert into smaller learning communities, such spaces can be assigned to individual SLCs to build ownership and community.

Outdoor spaces can refresh and reinvigorate a school's occupants. Overhanging roofs and awnings shade and protect outdoor corridors and offer spaces for outdoor study and relaxation.

In addition, shaded and well-protected outdoor areas can serve as classrooms in appropriate climates.

On sprawling campus layouts, outdoor gathering opportunities abound. Assigning such spaces to adjacent small learning communities – and enhancing them with benches, tables and landscaping designed to define and demarcate them from the larger campus – will optimize their use. The provision of shading structures can lend economical and dynamic visual elements that both identify and protect these spaces. When a community's indoor gathering or performance spaces open onto outdoor ones, the impulse redoubles to move from one space to the other, contributing to the feeling of small school as living community.

Outdoor spaces have another important function in a school: They lend dimension to the learning that goes on there. Shaded and well-protected areas can serve as classrooms in appropriate climates, but the outside world also provides its own instruction. Whether the school sits on a city block or in a cornfield, whether it overlooks a river or a freeway, the landscape offers endless opportunities for exploration and investigation. Its slopes, lawns, groves, trails, ponds, bogs, streams, bridges, parapets, and even gutters hold untold data for collection and analysis by kids who typically can't wait to get out there and mess around.

Schools can take advantage of their locations for instruction and learning. Nearby fields or ponds can provide resources for inquiry, research, and exploration.

Fieldwork in science classes provides the most common examples. Many teachers in small schools, for example, focus curriculum units on nearby water systems. Some schools purposely situate laboratories to have direct water access for hands-on projects; at least one has built a "mud room" to accommodate the slosh of boots and buckets as students leave and enter. The results of such field studies often benefit the community, providing important evidence for policy decisions concerning water quality. Just as important, participating in these projects trains young people to take their work seriously and do it carefully because their community needs it.

Other context-critical learning projects go outside the school doors to tackle real-world problems. Transportation systems, food and housing security, pest infestations, noise pollution, and access to city services all provide subjects for investigation and community action. A school's easy access to public places matters when it comes to getting students out doing observations, interviews, and other data collection.

▶ IN PRACTICE

Consider both the indoor and outdoor landscapes of your school as sites of active learning. Provide easy access from one to the other, designing spaces that invite discussion and exploration.

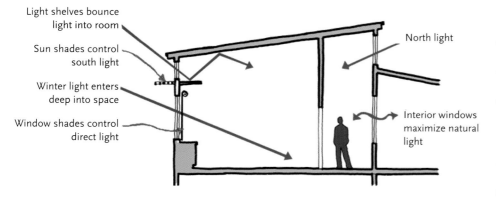

Light shelves bounce light into room

Sun shades control south light

Winter light enters deep into space

Window shades control direct light

North light

Interior windows maximize natural light

Light affects our motivation, energy, and vision – all of which profoundly connect to learning. Small schools recognize this when they design their dimensions and room arrangements to optimize natural light with artificial light in a balanced system made for long-term sustainability.

At left: Abundant glass in this museum school floods gathering spaces with light and provides a visual connection between the school and the surrounding public grounds.

Our bodies and spirits respond to the rhythms of day and night; too much time spent in artificial light erodes learning in subtle, but pernicious, ways. Confined in schools deprived of balanced daylight, students and adults alike complain of low energy levels, and recent studies confirm that learning rates improve when that deficiency is set right. Because the good small school regards the well-being of its community as a fundamental prerequisite for learning, it treats light as a key element in its building design.

Strategies for high quality daylight in schools begin with a clear understanding of the climate, geographical location, and the sun's trajectory across the sky

Windows with shading devices temper direct sunlight and allow indirect light into learning spaces.

at various times of the year. Initial building layout plays a key role, with the critical goal of ensuring that all learning spaces receive natural light. (This can prove useful in a power outage, because schools need not immediately cancel classes.) Designing wings for a building, with high, clerestory windows, will allow daylight to penetrate to its interior. In most locations, buildings oriented along an east-west axis allow for better control of daylight entering the structure. To avoid excessive heat and glare, school designers can temper light entering the south façade by overhangs, lattices, and reflective light shelves (interior or exterior shelves that shade spaces from direct light

A skylight runs along the entire length of this main corridor, bringing natural light into the building's core and highlighting the dynamic roof structure.

and reflect sunlight off the ceiling deep into the interior of a room). In the northern hemisphere, learning spaces can receive excellent light quality from indirect daylight on the north face of a building. Carefully designed skylights, clerestory windows, interior windows, light tunnels, or high transom windows also enhance the quality of light in the building by bringing light deep into the building's multi-story space.

Optimal light does not always come with an older building. Though many schools were initially built with ample daylight in mind, later generations may

Large window openings and a pendant fixture with lighting in two directions (downward for direct and upward for indirect light) provide abundant light to an informal reading and study area. Simple window blinds block direct sunlight while allowing for the adjustment of light levels throughout the day.

have covered exterior windows and windows on interior-facing doors – to conserve energy, to provide greater security, to compensate for poorly functioning blinds, or to minimize student distractions. Uncovering windows and replacing blinds can make a significant improvement. Adding larger windows to classroom doors contributes further to an environment conducive to learning.

All the important activities of the school day – reading, writing, working at computers, carrying out projects, performing and exhibiting work – require appropriate lighting levels to do attentively and well. However, that light need not always come at uniform intensity from a single source. Small task lights over local workstations can lend a feeling of focus to those at work. And light can help define an area where a small group meets, amplifying a sense of cohesiveness and purpose.

In addition to natural light from windows, the thoughtful design, selection, and control of light fixtures and shades can critically affect the quality of light in learning environments. With computers in almost every space, glare-free, even, and controllable light takes on even more importance. Schools need a balance of fixtures: those that send light upward to reflect off ceiling surfaces and those that direct light downward, directly onto the work surface. A good control system allows variable light levels within a room to accommodate a variety of learning activities. Mood lighting or unusual fixtures can also help give a distinct identity to a school or physical space within the building. These can be juxtaposed with simple incandescent lamp lighting, adding warmth to older buildings flooded with fluorescent light.

A school can both conserve energy and save money by balancing the daylight entering the school, selecting fixtures carefully, and installing well-designed controls for lighting throughout the building. The goal is a sustainable system that takes advantage of natural light whenever it is available, adding artificial light when needed to maintain consistent, high-quality ambient light at a lower operating cost.

▶ **IN PRACTICE**

Orient and design the rooms of your small learning community so they will be illuminated by indirect daylight. Supplement that light with artificial lighting and see that fixture design and control supports a variety of learning activities within a room.

16. Acoustic Balance

The wood panels on the walls of this music studio have a computer-designed pattern of holes drilled into them to provide an effective balance of sound reflection and absorption.

A small school community that values the individual voices of its members cannot function well without good acoustic balance in its spaces. The sounds of active learning can fill its building and grounds with a sense of vibrant collaboration and community. But learning also requires concentration and quiet, and so a design must strike the right balance between sound and silence.

The noise that pervades a conventional high school often drowns out the learning that might go on there. Students shout to each other in crowded corridors. The slams of locker doors reverberate down the hard surfaces of hallways and into classrooms. Teachers raise their voices to assert authority over large classes. Bells and announcements interrupt to blare messages at unpredictable moments. No wonder so many students walk about with headphones in their private worlds of music. As a result, more students than ever have trouble understanding what is said in class.

To maximize the use of this high-volume, multiple-purpose space, acoustics can be controlled by "tuning" the space with adjustable perimeter curtains (behind wood slats). General room acoustics can be handled with absorptive ceiling surfaces. Performances can be enhanced with an orchestra shell projecting sound into the space.

Good small schools, in contrast, seek to create the culture and physical conditions that respect the needs of each person to hear and be heard without losing the vibrant hum that signals active and purposeful learning. Starting early in the planning stages, school leaders are talking with architects and acoustical engineers about their values, plans, and expectations so as to achieve spatial acoustics that will respond appropriately to the learning activities they envision.

To achieve an environment with such acoustics, school-building designers must first ensure sound isolation from both interior and exterior sources of noise. By careful design and detailing of doors, windows, walls, and roofs, they can mitigate loud sounds from a nearby gym, music room, cafeteria, busy street, aircraft flight path, or construction zone. They must then reduce the reverberation time of sounds within each learning area (which greatly affects students' ability to recognize what is said) by balancing

Sound absorptive acoustic panels substantially soften ambient sound levels when students circulate hallways between classes.

absorptive room surfaces with the usual reflective wall, floor, and ceiling surfaces. In both these instances, they can call on criteria that professional acousticians have outlined for acceptable levels of noise in learning spaces.

In the interest of adaptability and flexibility, many schools design open environments with movable wall partitions to accommodate small and larger groups. These pose acoustic challenges, however, especially if teachers use the rooms for conventional instruction in voices that carry across partitioned areas.

Small schools seeking a more open learning environment must pay attention to keeping unwanted noise from reverberating throughout large spaces by controlling room volume and carefully positioning sound-absorbing materials. Although operable wall partitions provide spatial flexibility, they can introduce problems through inadequate quality, poor detailing, or inappropriate operation. Noisy mechanical systems can also have a negative impact, so designers must take care to carefully position heating and ventilating equipment with special attention to the layout, sizing, and detailing of air ducts.

Baffles and acoustic cubes keep sound from the large gathering space from disturbing the classroom wing above.

Sound quality is especially important when designing performance spaces, communications studios, or distance learning classrooms. Research has shown, for example, that sound is more critical than picture for remote instruction. Any room in which students and teacher communicate via an electronic connection must have well-designed acoustics and a good balance of speakers and microphone coverage. A few schools provide earphones and lapel microphones for distance learning in multipurpose rooms.

Good acoustics help establish the norm of mutual communication so important to a small school's culture, and also contribute to its commitment to meet the needs of diverse students. While all learners must be able to hear clearly to learn and communicate effectively, English language learners and students with disabilities are especially challenged in noisy classrooms. Increased environmental noise is also damaging children's hearing. In response to these challenges, some schools with a focus on direct instruction have installed classroom amplification systems via a mobile transmitter attached to a microphone, which sends the speaker's voice to a radio receiver that amplifies it by speakers throughout the room. Just as with distance learning, the existing physical layout and acoustics of a room can make or break this strategy.

Where possible, good small schools avoid delivering information to the entire community in a noisy, impersonal, or intrusive manner. Instead of one-way communication via a public address system, each classroom has a telephone and intercom connecting it to the school office. Classes break up when their time has come to an end, not with harsh bells or tones. These practices can result in a calmer and more respectful learning environment, lending an air of tranquility to even the most energetic high school.

▶ **IN PRACTICE**

Discuss the aural environment appropriate for your school, and design acoustically balanced learning spaces in which all can hear and be heard. Mitigate unwanted noise intrusion and excess reverberation through thoughtful detailing and construction practices. To control for sound reverberation, pay careful attention to the shape, volume, and materials used in the construction and finishes of the school. The type of learning that will occur in any given space will likely influence these variables.

Collaborative

The facility supports collaboration —
student-to-student, adult-to-student,
and adult-to-adult — and provides spaces
that facilitate high-quality interactions.
Families and community members
feel welcome, engaged, and involved.

17. Clusters of Learning

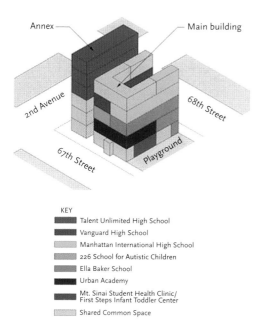

Annex — — Main building

2nd Avenue

68th Street

67th Street

Playground

KEY
- Talent Unlimited High School
- Vanguard High School
- Manhattan International High School
- 226 School for Autistic Children
- Ella Baker School
- Urban Academy
- Mt. Sinai Student Health Clinic/ First Steps Infant Toddler Center
- Shared Common Space

The six schools that co-inhabit this multiplex – previously a failing urban high school – each have their own contiguous spaces. All schools share the library, an art gallery, and some specialty classrooms.

At left: In this open plan, advisory learning nooks – located off of a common work area – support both independent learning and group activities.

Just as a school's academic program should not group together so many students that their teachers cannot know them well, its room arrangements should avoid a sense of mass production. Large high schools can organize themselves into autonomous small schools – under the same roof yet occupying separate spaces. Small high schools can create even smaller learning communities by clustering classrooms, teachers' offices, project rooms, conference rooms, and multipurpose spaces.

A hallway lined with classrooms through which masses of students circulated once stood as the physical symbol of our dominant educational philosophy. But calling on new understanding about how people learn, the best high schools now organize themselves along another design where teachers adapt instruction to students' needs, coaching them as they actively construct knowledge. This philosophical shift drives the movement for smaller high schools, and it also affects their building design.

When several small schools share a large building, an architect can cluster rooms to both symbolize and foster the autonomy each school must have.

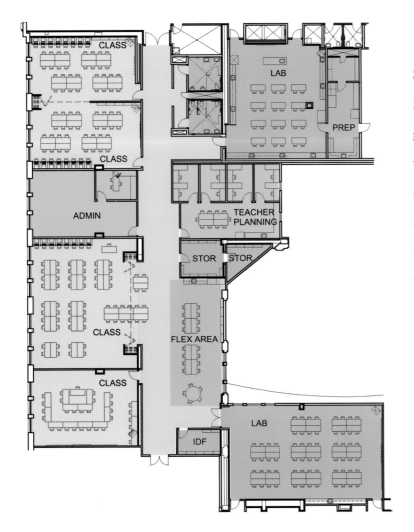

Similarly, when converting an existing high school into a multiplex of small schools, schools can be grouped in stand-alone buildings, in the horizontal wings of a structure, on several floors of a multistory building, or in a group of portables. Students and teachers entering their area of the school should have a physical sense that they belong within its boundaries and that its space can meet most of their needs. This sense may come from a variety of elements: separate entry and access to outdoor spaces; separate storage for student portfolios; and the ability to adapt structural, mechanical, or electrical systems to meet curricular needs. Such design decisions support the community-building essential to successful small schools, while protecting the individual character and culture each strives to develop.

When small learning communities are created within a large high school complex, contiguous space is crucial. Ideally, each cluster includes all SLC classrooms (including labs), an administrative office, teacher work room, and commons gathering space.

At the same time, a school has much to gain by thinking through which elements should occupy positions adjacent to each other. For example, a multiplex without the budget to construct separate science laboratories for each small-school cluster might decide to locate its labs in a core area adjoining all of the individual small schools.

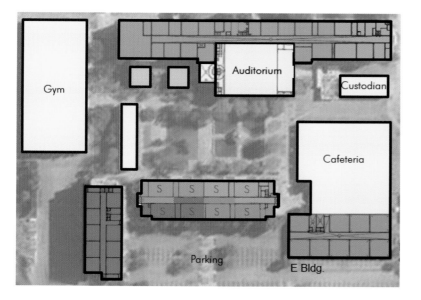

Gym

Auditorium

Custodian

Cafeteria

S S S S

S S S S

Parking

E Bldg.

Each small learning community on this once comprehensive high school campus has its own contiguous space on campus. However, given the permanence of science labs, all students take courses in the science building. To maintain small school identity and ownership, science labs are assigned to small learning communities, as seen in this illustration.

Depending on the particular science needs of the various programs, each small school could either "own" its individual labs or negotiate with other schools to share them.

Many schools in a multiplex situation also arrange for small schools to share lunchrooms, auditoriums, or gymnasiums. Students may like this practice, if it gives them the chance to see friends who attend other small schools in the building. But some schools prefer not to share a cafeteria, regarding eating lunch in the small community as a practice that contributes to a family atmosphere and a safer climate. Other schools choose to set aside their own spaces for small-scale performances or fitness activities. To support the autonomy a good small high school needs, a building design should strive to create the intimate feeling of a community, providing formal and informal spaces so that learning can take place in both academic and social settings.

Even a freestanding small school does well to arrange its learning spaces in clusters. A high school of 400 students increases its leverage over people and resources when it breaks its program and its building design into four clusters, each serving one hundred students and a team of teachers. This strategy both fosters collaboration and encourages personal attention to students.

This school's academic wing houses four "neighborhoods" of adjacent seminar rooms, studio spaces (pictured above), teachers' offices, conference rooms, project rooms, student lockers, and outdoor learning patios. These neighborhoods promote a sense of ownership and place.

Putting certain classrooms adjacent to each other also supports teachers in crossing subject-area boundaries or combining classes to integrate subjects. Decisions like this help a school depart from the factory model of schooling and engage students by personalizing their learning, focusing on issues important to them, and encouraging them to address complex questions from the real world. Establishing such adjacencies can be difficult in conversion projects, particularly with science and specialty labs. Many schools have preserved small school autonomy while still allowing students to take courses in small learning communities other than their own by assigning these "crossover" courses to classrooms located on the fringes of small learning communities.

▷ **IN PRACTICE**

Think of the spaces in your high school as clusters of adjacent rooms that house small communities, which can break into even smaller groups to afford a variety of settings for learning. When several small schools share a facility, design it to support each school's autonomy.

18. Gathering Spaces

This open studio space creates a "family room" atmosphere where a wide variety of learning activities occur throughout the school day.

For a school to be a genuine learning community, it needs places to gather. There its members can envision and develop the common focus so important to a small school's success; they can work through the issues that face them in a democratic fashion; they can show their work and subject it to critique; and they can celebrate or reflect together. The arenas where a learning community gathers can support all these needs if their design adapts easily to gatherings both large and small, or to large gatherings that may break into smaller groups and then reassemble.

In traditional high school designs, the community typically gathers in a large auditorium or gymnasium facing forward passively, with acoustics that often make it hard to hear those presenting information to the group. Small schools have found that this model can hamper democratic participation and group inquiry. They are looking instead for new places to join together, where people can see and be heard and where the relationships between presenter and audience can be interactive.

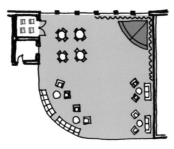

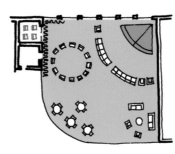

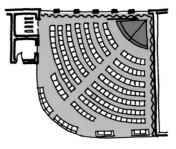

Informal Gatherings   Small Group Gatherings   Large Group Presentations

The places where a learning community gathers can support a variety of needs if the design adapts easily to gatherings both large and small, or to large gatherings that may break into smaller groups and then reassemble.

This can mean a "great room," cafeteria, commons, or hall – adaptable spaces that can both embrace a large group and invite smaller groups to find their voices and strengthen their bonds. Such a place can serve as both the cultural hub of the school and its intellectual heart. Much community gathering focuses on food, and even though some schools encourage eating in smaller groupings, many still gather in large community spaces to have lunch together. Portable staging or risers might serve as elements of such an area without limiting its use for non-performance situations. Parts of the space could temporarily adapt as needed – for example, to create a backdrop for the exhibition and presentation of student work, or to open onto the outdoors, or to shield a section from view and provide more intimacy. A great room could also provide space for students to work together on projects, or it might serve as a commons where students just hang out.

This school's "great hall" is used as a lunch room, assembly room, and performance hall. A portable stage, collapsible stadium seating, and acoustic devices (including curtains and sound-reflective panels) create a flexible space, capable of meeting a variety of needs as they arise.

Many large high schools lack dispersed, adaptable spaces for small learning community gatherings. One solution is to convert classrooms located near small-school entries or reception areas into commons spaces. If this is not feasible, some schools make use of shared spaces in which larger groups can gather, meet, present, and exhibit their work, even if only for a prescribed period of time. Underutilized shop areas, for example, possess ample space for community gathering; and by remodeling fixed-seat auditoriums with telescoping seats and a stepped floor surface, one can better accommodate smaller meetings. (When several small schools share gathering spaces such as auditoriums, however, the building's occupants must carefully negotiate schedules, security, and maintenance.)

Small school communities can also gather in shaded outdoor areas, as weather permits. In the tradition of a village commons, outdoor stages, amphitheaters, and courtyards provide centrally located areas in which to congregate. Designating an outdoor commons for each small learning community on a larger campus can help compensate for the lack of indoor gathering opportunities.

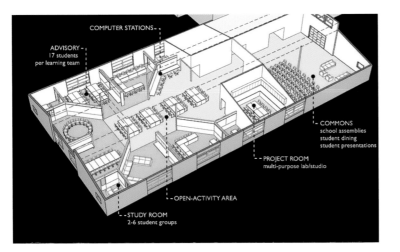

In this small school design for approximately 100 students, advisory spaces, study and project rooms, and computer work areas all open on to an open activity area, which is utilized in a wide variety of ways throughout the school day.

This large-group gathering area is placed and designed to take full advantage of the building's historic architectural features.

The design of a small school's gathering place may emerge from its history as well as its values. One school made its home in a landmark building that once housed an auto dealership on a central thoroughfare of the city. Its grand showroom, resplendent with Corinthian columns and coffered ceiling, became a place where the community gathered to forge its future in a new era.

Smaller gathering places also foster a school's culture of inquiry, collaboration, personalization, and democracy. One small school clusters several classrooms around a common "studio" where groups can gather for meetings, presentations, practices, or performances. Another has organized itself in a daisy pattern, with the center used as a common gathering space for learning communities of 100 students, and the "petals" as space for advisory and work groups.

▶ **IN PRACTICE**

Create spaces where groups of different sizes – including the whole community – can gather. In its design, strive to further your small school's goal of knowing all its members, honoring their contributions, and respecting every voice.

19. Professional Work Areas

Teacher collaboration areas, when designed with transparency in mind, can allow students to witness adults as learners and professional colleagues.

A small school's culture of high standards, respect, collaboration, and warmth depends on its teachers and staff, and their professional work spaces ought to convey those same qualities. To reach that objective, teachers must have enough room to work both undisturbed and with others, in a location that encourages contact with students and offers office amenities that facilitate efficiency and communication.

Addressing the nation's shortage of good high school teachers might easily start with raising the quality of their professional workspaces. Too often, teachers must crowd into cramped and depressing quarters without telephones or other standard office equipment. Lacking a quiet and congenial place to meet, they struggle to have collegial conversations about their teaching practice. And the placement of their offices often indicates the school's fortress mentality rather than its expectation that teachers will make themselves easily available to students and community members.

To strike a better balance in the work lives of teachers, small schools can design spaces that respect their need to think and plan, focus and connect,

In order to maximize classroom usage, each academy in this multiplex has a teacher room with individual work space, tables for common planning and collaboration, teacher resources, and storage space.

at the same time staying accessible to students. A group of workstations set apart by windowed walls, for example, could facilitate communication within a particular team or sector of teachers while protecting against intrusive noise. Students might see teachers at work there and seek them out, while teachers could retreat from more crowded areas and simultaneously maintain connection with the ebb and flow of the school's human rhythms.

Communication lies at the heart of teaching, and we should equip teachers with all the tools they need to do it well: a telephone for outside calls; a computer with high-speed Internet access; easy access to a printer, fax, and copier; voice messaging. Other professionals take these things for granted, and so should teachers.

When teachers confer with colleagues, students, or parents, they need privacy to speak without being overheard. Clusters of workspaces could include a table large enough to accommodate a team of teachers and a small meeting space for private conversations. Comfortable seating in such areas may seem like a minor matter, but it can contribute to establishing a tone of good will and professional conduct.

In overcrowded, large high school settings, small learning communities must get creative in locating central areas for teacher work and collaboration. Some schools convert departmental offices; others free up certain classrooms by more fully using the others. Rather than being "owned" by individual

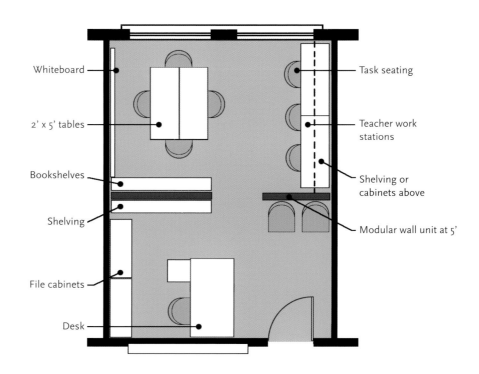

Whiteboard

2' x 5' tables

Bookshelves

Shelving

File cabinets

Desk

Task seating

Teacher work stations

Shelving or cabinets above

Modular wall unit at 5'

A small teacher work room, when well designed, can include individual workstations, a collaboration area, a resource library, and storage.

teachers, in cases like this classrooms shift from "me" space to "we" space. Teachers will share classrooms more readily when they receive in exchange a dedicated space in which they can confer and retreat.

Space for the faculty to meet as a whole has equal importance. A professional community becomes too large, small school leaders believe, when it cannot come together easily in one room to participate in democratic decisions. That room's design and furnishings should make it easy to hear and be heard, to take notes that all can see, to view media presentations, to listen and respond to speakers, and to break out for small discussions and then regroup.

A teacher development center, shared by several small
schools in the building, provides space for collaboration,
and serves as a professional development library.

Teachers at a small high school take responsibility for much more than instruction. They lead change efforts, collaborate with colleagues, plan curriculum, assess student work, supervise projects, interact with parents, and connect their students with the outside world, among many other things. They are continually on call, coaching, advising, tutoring, prodding, and encouraging their students. Often they spend most of their waking hours at work, and the design of their workplace should acknowledge and support them. Because small schools are first and foremost about personalization, workplaces should invite student-teacher interactions and collaboration. In addition, some schools may design places in the school for teachers to retreat and rest, put their feet up, or sit quietly with a cup of tea before their next interaction with students. We will have the teachers that our schools so desperately need when we show them that we value their work. The design of their workplace plays an important part in that.

▷ **IN PRACTICE**

Review all the expectations your small high school has of its teachers and staff, and then design their professional work areas to support those activities. Keep in mind that a teacher's duties span the spectrum from solitary concentration to large-group collaboration. Among these, however, connection with students is primary; let that priority show in the places where teachers work.

Community-Connected

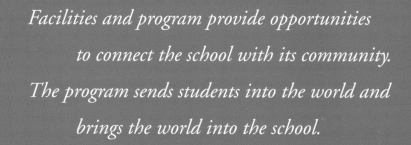

Facilities and program provide opportunities to connect the school with its community. The program sends students into the world and brings the world into the school.

20. Siting in Context

An entire neighborhood can be revitalized when a magnificent school building is placed in its midst.

At left: This rural school, intimately set in the Nebraska cornfields, emphasizes community and interdisciplinary cross-grade learning.

How and where a school sits in its surrounding landscape conveys a great deal about its purposes and its priorities. It can evoke connections not only with the past and present uses of its geographical site, but also with the cultures, purposes, and aspirations of the people who gather there for learning.

Through its siting, a small school can express continuity with the land-use traditions of the place it serves. Whether students and teachers come together in an urban setting (such as a school situated in a former automobile showroom on a busy Boston thoroughfare), a rural landscape (such as a Nebraska school set in the midst of cornfields), or an industrial zone (such as a Seattle school focused on aviation, located near an airstrip), the school's placement reminds everyone of its priorities and provides an entry to profound learning about local history and culture.

In times past, high schools often sent a message of grandeur through their size and placement. Set high on a hill or secluded behind walls, such buildings were intended to inspire lofty aspirations for the school's learners. A community's pride in its high school – an institution as important as the church in bringing a community together – often showed up in its choice of a setting that evoked respect and even devotion. Yet over time, that symbolism eroded. Often schools now operate as if they are set apart from the community at large, keeping students cloistered within their walls during the school day.

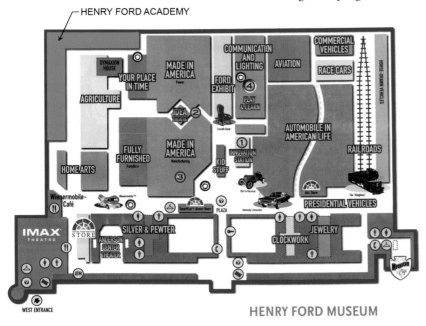

Located in an industrial museum, this small school calls on that institution's rich resources for hands-on, experiential learning and internships.

These days, rather than retreating from the community, many small high schools are reaching into it, reflecting a new philosophy of learning that emphasizes connections with the adult world. In this regard, a high school's location can literally open doors to opportunity. Thoughtful siting can make it easy for students and faculty to gain access to and develop partnerships with the community and its cultural, educational, and civic institutions, and for the community to enter the school to use its resources. Mentoring relationships, apprenticeships, field studies, and connections to higher education all gain from a site that makes it easy to send students into the world and to bring the world into the school.

If several small schools share space in a larger school building, the building can situate them to best use the resources and types of spaces that each separate program requires. Unless security concerns preclude it, one could organize separate entrances, drop-off points, and parking zones to signal each school's

Designing this campus as a series of three-story buildings reduces the building footprints and maximizes the preservation of existing trees and understory. Buildings are oriented to accommodate the site's steep grade changes, harvest natural daylight, and capture water and landscape views.

autonomy and separate identity. In new construction, the building spaces that small schools share – auditoriums, gymnasiums, and the like – can be placed near major entrances, sheltering more separate and autonomous learning areas from the busy public interface.

Siting decisions also can express how environmental factors prompt student learning at a small school. At a school with a project-based curriculum, students often take advantage of the surrounding urban or natural landscapes to investigate real-world problems that cross the academic disciplines. When the school site invites such connections, it enriches and enlarges the curriculum in important way, providing a real-world context for learning.

▶ **IN PRACTICE**

Know the history and culture of the place your school will occupy and explore the ways they connect to the lives and aspirations of those who will learn there. Make those connections apparent to anyone who approaches the building from outside, and let them show up in the academic program as well.

21. Community Resources

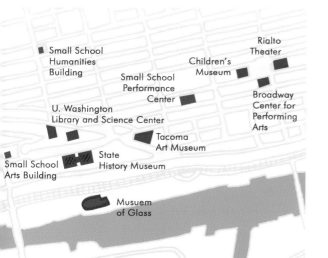

Small School Humanities Building

Children's Museum

Rialto Theater

Small School Performance Center

U. Washington Library and Science Center

Broadway Center for Performing Arts

Tacoma Art Museum

State History Museum

Small School Arts Building

Musuem of Glass

This small school uses its downtown location to take advantage of local resources. Nearby museums, university classrooms, businesses, and even a light rail system share their facilities with the school.

At left: Adjunct artists enrich student experiences at this small arts school. As local artists share their talents and experience in specialized course offerings, student learning becomes more authentic.

The small high school's design should reflect a lively give-and-take with its community, both within the school and outside it. Sharing resources within the building establishes norms of mutual support that strengthen the bonds among those who work and learn there. Going beyond the walls, students and teachers can explore and make use of community resources while sharing their own facilities and expertise with the larger community, to the benefit of all.

By taking every opportunity to bring community members into the school and students into the community, many small high schools have made great strides in breaking down the walls that separate school and community. School and community can share in the use of resources such as cafeterias, libraries, gymnasiums, theaters, clinics, art studios, technology labs, conference facilities, and exhibition spaces. Community-based organizations can become formal partners, contributing to and sharing the vision and design of the school. In one Seattle-area multiplex, numerous social service agencies have established satellite offices in a centrally located building

Students at this urban school have become a vital and vibrant part of the city's burgeoning downtown community. As they use public transportation to move between the school's various downtown locations, students prepare for future civic involvement.

within the school; as community members visit the school complex for services, it functions as a community hub.

Neighborhoods flourish when schools within them thrive. As the community develops a sense of the school's values, goals, and needs, it begins to contribute more resources to help the school succeed. Student work benefits from exposure to an outside eye, partly because this helps students realize its importance and partly because outside expertise can bring important new perspectives. Through internships and field studies, the community can also draw on the energy and talent of high school students. More important, when students are given opportunities to develop relationships with mentors in the community, they gain access to the adult world of work and learning they are poised to enter.

A school fosters such relationships when it designates clearly accessible areas in the school to support community connections and facilitates navigation through the school with posted maps and signs. Tutors or mentors, parent volunteers or aides, and invited speakers or experts will feel more welcome and at ease if they have places to sit down with a cup of coffee, review materials describing the school and its program, talk with staff or students,

Schools and communities can find many opportunities for resource sharing and collaboration. In this school, community members have been invited to use the new library and technology center, and many of them have volunteered to serve as mentors to students.

Simple signage can go a long way in encouraging adult involvement in the life of a small school.

check their email, and make a phone call. This can take place in a range of settings: small conference rooms, mobile workstations, the corner of a commons area or library, or an office dedicated specifically for use by outside visitors.

The increased interconnectedness between school and community can also present challenges in the design of a school's building and grounds. Some space might be reserved for the exclusive use of a particular program, for example, while other space is shared or co-owned. When it comes to sharing facilities, all parties should clearly detail in writing their agreement on issues

KING COUNTY
BOYS AND GIRLS CLUB

CITY PARK

THE
TRUMAN
CENTER

HEADSTART
CHILDCARE

Above and at right: By building a small school in conjunction with an adjacent Head Start childcare center and a Boys and Girls Club, planners created a small learning village. Facilities are shared and students are able to take advantage of rich internship and after-school opportunities.

such as access and security, cleanup and maintenance responsibilities, and storage of equipment and materials. They should then maintain and revisit these formal agreements or memorandums of understanding in ways that nurture and respect the evolving needs of the school and its community partners.

Small schools that share facilities in a larger building can also face challenges. Although common spaces might be shared by several small schools in a building, it is important to create autonomous spaces in which each small school can develop its unique sense of identity and build its own culture and community. Different staffs often find themselves competing for areas designated for common use, such as performance space or gymnasiums. Building designers can mitigate such problems by providing flexible and adaptable spaces within the small school's boundaries so that people have options when someone else is using a space they need.

Forging strong bonds with others who share the building has lasting positive effects. Leaders lay the groundwork for respectful behavior among their students and teachers when they create opportunities for the building's occupants to come together and resolve governance issues, share their challenges and accomplishments, and celebrate.

▷ **IN PRACTICE**

Provide resources that your school can share with the outside public and look for community resources the school can use as well. Make outsiders welcome in the small school by giving them places to easily observe, interact, contribute, work, and debrief. Anticipate the tensions of living in community and develop spaces and systems that offer the flexibility to meet the challenges of a vibrant, evolving small school culture.

Adaptable and Flexible

Education and the world are evolving rapidly. Facilities are flexible and adaptable enough to support a range of educational program models — including those not yet identified.

22. Multi-Use Classrooms

In contrast to a traditional classroom, designed for stand-and-deliver instruction, this learning space is zoned for individual, small-group, and large-group projects. Learning remains fluid and the teacher can coach students in an individualized manner.

At left: A variety of furniture, adequate lighting, sound-absorptive tiles, and a sink allow this classroom to be used in diverse ways throughout the day.

People learn in many different ways, and the design of classrooms in a good small high school reflects that. Their spaces adapt easily to a variety of teaching and learning styles, providing multiple settings in which students can develop skills and knowledge, collaborate, and make their work public. Classrooms are more than empty boxes; their strategic use can include a broad range of learning activities, such as student projects, community meetings, lectures, presentations, and exercise. Key adjacencies with other specialty rooms and areas can further extend the use of these multipurpose spaces.

The stereotype of a high school classroom has twenty or thirty desks in neat rows with a teacher behind the desk at the front. Students listen while the teacher delivers information, writes on the board, or asks and answers questions. Most of the students' work takes place as they sit at their desks reading from their textbooks, writing in their notebooks, raising their hands, and occasionally dozing off.

We typically still call a classroom a classroom, but a good small school uses it in "non-classroom" ways. More often, one will find students gathered

Hands-on projects, experiments, creative expression, and other learning experiences require flexible classrooms that offer adequate room for collaboration, storage for supplies and works-in-progress, and expansive work surfaces.

around tables in dialogue, or at a computer workstation, or constructing a model, or heading off to an interview, or on their feet presenting their research in a mixed-media project. The textbook has given way to active exploration of information-age resources; the notebook plays only a supporting part in presentations of learning.

What kind of space fosters learning like this? Flexible furniture allows two-person tables to be easily placed in neat rows for direct instruction, or paired for four students to work together, or configured in a U-shape for seminars, or arranged in a wide variety of other ways. The chalkboard would be replaced by a whiteboard, an LCD projector with a white wall or screen, or even a "smart board" combining the power of a projector and a computer. Computer workstations or wireless laptops with high-speed connections would help students develop and practice skills in research, writing, or mathematical modeling.

Such a room might have more nooks and crannies, so that small groups could break away. Similar to many elementary-level rooms, classrooms could be zoned to accommodate a variety of activities; L-shaped classrooms work particularly well for this purpose. An operable wall or partition might move to combine two classrooms for team teaching, project work, and presentations. Tables and storage carts could move easily out of the way to clear space for a project or a presentation. A display wall could open to reveal cabinets; a ledge could turn into a stage.

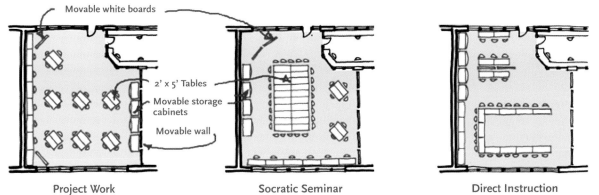

Movable white boards

2' x 5' Tables

Movable storage cabinets

Movable wall

Project Work   **Socratic Seminar**   **Direct Instruction**

Instructional approaches can change from day-to-day and period-to-period when furniture is flexible and portable.

In conversion schools, classrooms with sinks allow physics or biology instruction to be imbedded in a small learning community's area of campus. Portable sink systems and self-venting portable fume-hoods could also allow additional classrooms to be used for science as necessary. Old shop space could provide rich opportunities for hands-on learning and rooms of varied sizes could accommodate an array of learning activities. Replacing traditional, clunky "tablet arm" desks with movable and stackable tables and chairs can make space more adaptable.

The multi-use classroom has good light, but it can go dark when that serves a purpose. Its acoustics honor a whisper, a speech, or a song. It assures safety and can even offer comfort, but its design also supports risk and effort and dignifies accomplishment in all its various forms.

▷ **IN PRACTICE**

Look for opportunities for flexibility in design choices, so as to transform the classroom into a place of active learning. Imagine several ways students and teachers could use each element in the classroom, and how it could adapt to different learning styles.

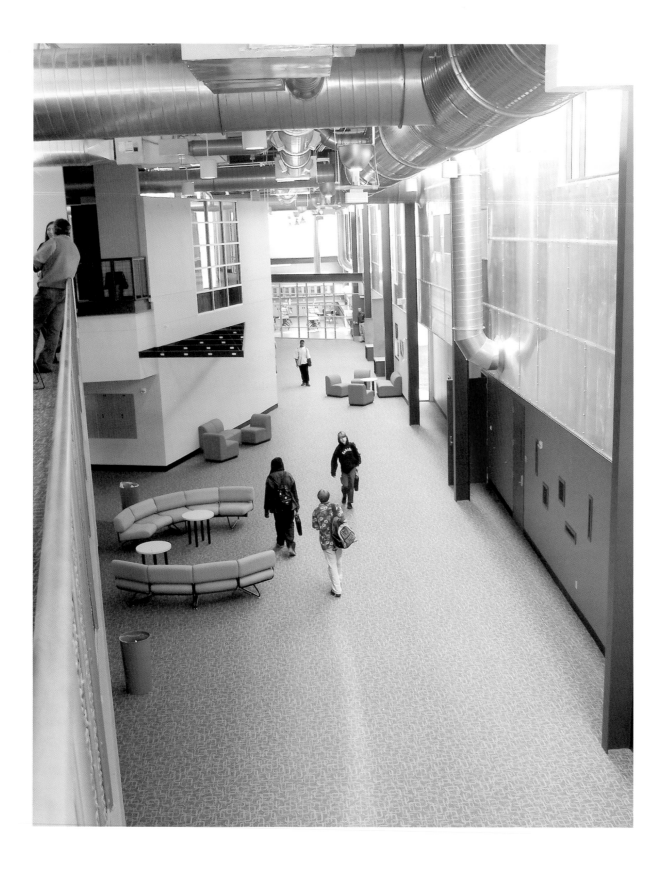

23. Learning Supports: Furniture and Storage

Movable furniture that can be configured in a variety of arrangements is preferable to stationary desks, which limit teaching and learning approaches.

At left: Soft, movable, brightly colored seating and coffee tables invite informal gatherings in this gallery space, the school's main circulation spine.

The small school community supports learning wherever it occurs. Furniture and storage play key roles in that commitment. Indoors or outdoors, in enclosed rooms and common areas, wherever students and teachers gather they should find comfortable seating, work surfaces, and smart storage that can be flexibly configured to help advance their purposes.

Our memories of high school often take place against the backdrop of a room full of desks with metal legs, plastic seats, and a tablet arm on which to write. In rows, they faced the teacher's desk, and along with blackboards and shelving, they constituted the sole furnishings of almost every classroom. Laboratories had high stools and work tables; teachers' rooms had large tables stacked with materials; cafeterias were filled with long tables with benches attached; hallways were lined with metal lockers. Comfort did not qualify as a condition for learning; a school's reputation for rigor and the economical use of public funds derived partly from its spartan furniture and cold locker bays.

But the more personal, flexible, and respectful qualities of a good small high school often show up in the ordinary evidence of its everyday furnishings.

Lightweight, stackable chairs and study tables on casters are often moved aside in this studio space to allow for learning cluster presentations and meetings.

In the classroom, students might sit in pairs at rectangular tables (60 inches wide by 24 inches deep) that they can also push together to make larger tables for projects or a U-shape for seminars. Chairs should move easily across a quiet, resilient floor surface, stacking when necessary to clear the room. Classroom furniture should be made of good materials, sturdy enough to resist damage, yet lightweight enough to pick up and move around. Its ergonomic design should make it inviting and comfortable for both students and adults.

Throughout the learning environment, one might find work surfaces with ample electrical wiring for technology and room to spread out work materials. When teachers share classrooms, their storage spaces can be individualized. Some schools build storage walls in their classrooms, with lockable doors that double as whiteboards. While built-in storage cabinets and millwork may provide efficient storage and might be less expensive initially, they can also limit flexibility and take up valuable square footage. Movable storage units, including wardrobe-sized cabinets for each teacher in a shared classroom, can serve as room dividers and enable more substantial and timely reconfiguration of the classroom when desired.

Well designed and thoughtfully placed backpack hooks can eliminate the need for lockers, which increases security and provides students with easy access to their learning resources.

For security and maintenance reasons, many schools no longer assign lockers to individual students. In classrooms, tables and desks might be outfitted with sturdy recessed hooks on which a heavy backpack can hang. If advisory groups serve as students' home base during the school day, a school might put a bank of individual drawers or compartments for students in each advisory space. When students with outsized, heavy, or valuable equipment – from lacrosse sticks to laptop computers – need storage of varying sizes, short-term lockers can be made available to students as needed. Placing such lockers in each small school, as opposed to placement in a common area of campus, helps build autonomy and small school identity, and increases security through ownership and proximal location. Unused locker bays can be replaced with display cases to showcase student work.

Schools are solving the storage problems of teachers who share classrooms by providing a variety of solutions including bookcases, secure cabinets, and wardrobes that are light-weight, portable, and lockable.

Some small schools prefer a separate, secure room in which to store all student portfolios and projects. These storerooms can be equipped with shelves that teachers customize to hold everything from disks to dioramas or drawings. Basements or attics could be outfitted with chain-link storage units (as in some apartment buildings) to accommodate seldom-used supplies over the long term. Some schools even opt for the ongoing use of commercial storage facilities on an as-needed basis.

A separate room may also be necessary to store stackable chairs and folding tables for use in commons areas. Alternatively, some schools use seating that folds up into the walls when not in use. Others look for imaginative ways to store large equipment; wrestling mats, for example, can hang from the rafters of a gymnasium.

More and more often, schools are providing their teachers with professional office spaces that include group planning areas, individual workstations, storage cabinets, telephone lines, data hook-ups, and computers. When office spaces are not located adjacent to classrooms, teachers need a table surface or desktop in the classroom to temporarily set up shop. Other schools go the more traditional route of locating teachers in their own class-rooms, providing workstations and storage within the room itself. Still other schools are virtual and network-based. Students and teachers have dedicated work folders that allow them to share files and information and collaborate

To save space and provide shelving, this small school built storage walls in its classrooms with lockable doors that double as whiteboards. The doors slide back to reveal shelves and cubbies for use by a particular class.

from home or any location with computer access, decreasing the need for both storage and physical space. Regardless of configuration, student learning spaces should be protected against the encroachment of large teacher desks, filing cabinets, and projects waiting to be assessed.

Throughout the school, furniture and storage decisions help express the ethos of the school – welcome and inclusiveness at the entry, comfort and consideration in the lounge and reading area, and activity and purpose in the learning areas. Round tables in the lunchroom lend a convivial, family-like tone; in appropriate locations, couches and easy chairs afford moments of collegiality and respite.

Even the materials, color, and style of furnishings – particularly when they reflect a small school's overall visual identity – help convey the school's philosophy and priorities and, in a large campus, assist with wayfinding. Tables with wheels or skids speak to a belief in flexibility and change; stable and sturdy work platforms in shops and labs demonstrate a commitment to safety. Corporate donations of used furnishings in good condition offer evidence of healthy community relationships. Schools might invest in more adaptable systems furnishings even though they can cost more than less flexible, built-in systems. Some small schools enlist the artistic talents of students to put their individual or collective stamp on school furnishings.

The thoughtful choice of furnishings can have both physical and psychological effects on students and adults in a small school. Appropriate, ergonomically designed seating and surfaces in work areas help combat the physiological stress of a long day that requires frequent and rapid shifts from one task or position to another. The chance to gather comfortably in small groups for either work or relaxation also contributes to a culture of collaboration and trust. New furniture in recently converted small learning community classrooms and common areas helps teachers and students feel valued and sends the message that important changes have occurred. Finally, when furniture reflects an attitude of professionalism and respect toward the people who use it, everybody takes more responsibility for keeping it in good condition.

▶ **IN PRACTICE**

Equip your school with comfortable, sturdy furniture that teachers and students can move around to suit their learning needs. Plan for accessible and adaptable storage at several levels: for individuals, for smaller and larger groups, and for the whole school. Make sure all furnishings and storage solutions contribute to a culture that values individuality, collaboration, and mutual respect.

24. Flexible Boundaries

Operable wall partitions allow one teacher to easily address two classrooms of students, which facilitates teacher collaboration and interdisciplinary teaching and learning.

When it is founded, a small school often cannot predict how its use of space might change in the future as it adds more students or revises its academic program. However, it can stay open to new possibilities by making its boundaries flexible – architecturally, structurally, mechanically, and electrically. Without too much advance notice or technical expertise, people in the school should have the ability to expand some spaces or make them smaller to serve the learning needs of the community.

Boundaries protect us and unite us – in school communities as in life. The small school makes a statement by delineating its boundaries: This is where we learn together as a community and where we know each person well. When a large school divides into several learning communities, those involved care a great deal how its space is allocated. And even within the limited physical layout of a freestanding small school, people negotiate carefully about who gets what space and why.

To complicate matters, early scenarios that envision what will happen in a school often get revised as its operational needs evolve. A large school might

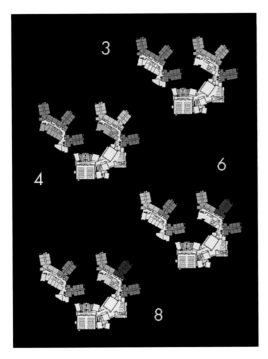

This school's flexible and adaptable design allows for as few as three and as many as eight small learning communities within the larger campus.

At right: These diagrams illustrate how one educational cluster can easily be converted to support a variety of educational program models.

start by breaking into four schools, for example, then increase or decrease that number as years go by. The theme and focus of a small learning community might evolve to address emergent student needs and community priorities. Teachers in a small school might decide to work in teams or to disband them; the arts curriculum might temporarily require more space; the school might decide to gather younger students in a separate section of the building. Space designed for use today may shift quickly as new technologies emerge.

Such revisions form one of the fundamental strengths and principles of a small school, which always stands ready to adapt in order to serve its students better. Whatever building the school occupies, it should be able to support that adaptation as well. Early on, school planners should explore multiple scenarios to ensure that a building's structural, electrical, mechanical, and plumbing systems can adapt to meet its future program needs.

For a campus that will house multiple small schools, designers often propose separate buildings for each. While such a design does help create autonomous schools (and may establish a "gone so far you can't go back" mentality), it can inhibit future flexibility. Adaptations are challenging, though possible, when four buildings – built for groups of equal size – need to house a different configuration in the future.

In a well-designed school building, people can make some changes on the spur of the moment without any structural alterations at all. They might

Academy

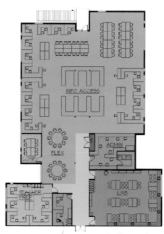

Independent

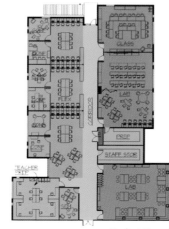

Project-Based

School-Within-a-School

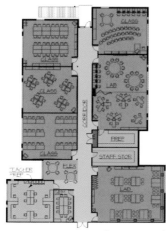

Departmental

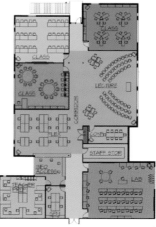

Integrated

Above and at right: This school employs garage-style and interior rolling doors to maximize space use. Learning spaces can easily grow or contract as needed.

pull a curtain to create a partition in a commons area or slide a movable wall back on its tracks to join two classes for a lecture or exhibition. Other changes, though, require more planning. For example, some schools use a demountable wall system, lining up their walls on a ceiling grid. With a day's warning, the walls can moved in two-foot increments, essentially redesigning the building to suit new needs.

The ability to divide and merge spaces has great value in schools where teachers work in teams, classes break into small groups, or project work requires flexible configurations. But such flexibility comes at a price. Good space dividers cost more than regular walls, for one thing, because high quality detailing, which seals the divider around its perimeter, is critical to effective acoustic separation. Less expensive dividers, six-foot walls, or even portable screens can prove useful when acoustic separation is less critical.

Once they become more comfortable with reconfiguring their spaces, some teachers take even small opportunities to move rolling storage units or portable screens so as to create large and small zones for a particular task. Without seeing their colleagues in action or understanding and using space dividers, other teachers may have trouble maximizing them. Some schools spend years in their building with movable walls without anyone using them. Teachers and staff need clear explanations and training concerning just what it takes to adapt their spaces in support of their curriculum. Occasional visits with staff to explore their needs and suggest possible

adaptations could also provide helpful reminders of their continuing power to create the school they need.

Seeking ways to configure these systems so they will support a school through the many possible evolutions in its future, a building's designers need more than technical expertise. They need to incorporate the vision and imagination of educators who look beyond how teaching and learning has been, and toward how it might be some day.

One caution: In conversion projects, some may view flexibility as an "escape route." If few structural changes occur, people say, it will be easier to change back to a more traditional high school model when challenges arise. Such thinking saps courageous transformation. While the existing campus organizer (such as the quad or central spine) may naturally limit some major renovations, reform best succeeds when schools go so far that they can't turn back. Sacrificing some flexibility to achieve commitment to fundamental change is a good tradeoff.

▶ **IN PRACTICE**

Imagine your school at its beginning and then think of all the ways it might need to change in the future. Design its building systems so they can adapt to evolving needs and then teach those in the school how to carry out those changes when the time comes, encouraging them to brainstorm their own visions of what could be.

25. Adaptable Utilities

Teachers have immediate control of their environment in this school's classroom pods. Operable windows and sliding glass doors into classrooms provide fresh air and cross-ventilation. The shared activity area within the pod has views to the forest and allows natural light to flood the space.

Just as users of a small school ought to be able to change a school's boundaries to suit their teaching and learning needs, so the building's utilities and technology infrastructure should be equally adaptable. Designers should think ahead about heating and ventilation, plumbing, electrical wiring, and lighting systems that they can adapt to a variety of possible uses, both present and future.

People need control over their own comfort in the small school workplace. Simple things such as opening a window, turning down the heat, or adjusting the lights can make a big difference in how well people teach and learn, how collegial and empowered they feel. The design of utility systems in a small school should take such realities into account by creating adjustable zones that allow people to control the amount of heat and lighting in their immediate environment.

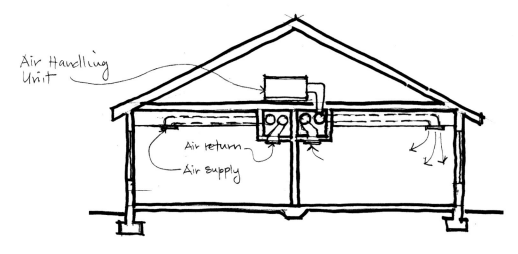

Air Handling Unit

Air return

Air supply

Provide mechanical systems (air handling, duct work, and controls) that can be reconfigured to support multiple learning-space layouts.

Over time, the same principle of adaptable utilities also applies. A small school might begin with one vision of how to use its spaces and then change as the years go by. What begins as an art room with a couple of sinks may someday be pressed into service as a biology laboratory, for example. A large open atrium in an educational complex housing several small schools may be used primarily as the school's cafeteria and drop-in study center. But with appropriate furnishings, adjustable lighting, partitions, and acoustic tuning, the space may be adapted to provide a place where students can meet in advisory groups or with mentors, play amplified instruments, or hold a dance with strobe lighting. Such changes are all part of the life and development of a school, and they cannot be precisely predicted.

From the start, however, one can lay pipes, cables, ducts, and wiring with the most ample possible vision of what a school may one day require. When the science teacher comes to the facilities manager in ten years and asks to add a

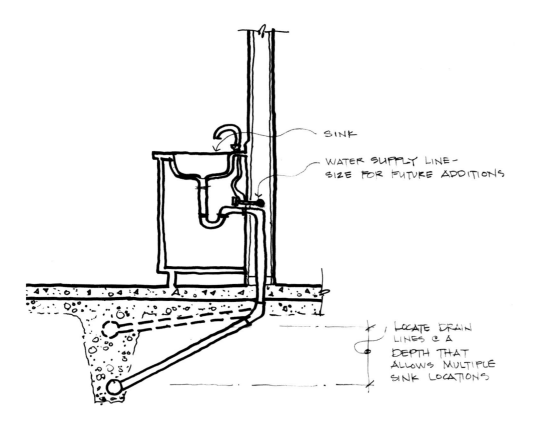

SINK

WATER SUPPLY LINE -
SIZE FOR FUTURE ADDITIONS

LOCATE DRAIN
LINES @ A
DEPTH THAT
ALLOWS MULTIPLE
SINK LOCATIONS

When sizing and locating supply and drain lines, a steeper pitch in drainage lines will increase future capacity, allowing more sinks to be added to the same line.

sink, the change will be more easily made if a wide range of future options has been anticipated in the original design. (One school buried its utility lines one to two feet deeper to facilitate possible future plumbing changes by maximizing drainage capacity.) When an increased power demand arises, prior planning should eliminate the need for major rewiring; the school's electrical design should already have anticipated the increased loads.

Decisions like this can add initial expense, but in the long run they have the potential to save considerable money, time, and aggravation. Like clothes, utilities make a better investment if one follows the maxim "Long life, loose fit." Contingency planning or creating scenarios for the future during the planning phase can minimize the need for a major retrofit later.

Floor-imbedded electrical and data outlets such as these acknowledge a building's fluid utility requirements.

Should a retrofit be necessary, as is often the case in conversion projects, it is crucial to understand the structural, mechanical, and electrical infrastructure and its opportunities for adaptive reuse. The type and location of existing facilities will have an impact on the ability to remove non-bearing walls in order to create small learning community gathering spaces, to convert an existing shop or studio to support science, or to turn a regular classroom into a technology-rich space.

▷ **IN PRACTICE**

Design zoned environmental controls that are simple enough for those in your school to use in creating a comfortable work setting. On the larger scale, think and plan for both current and future needs in the design of utility systems. Locate these so that they are accessible and adaptable to possible future uses you can envision and afford.

26. *Living Buildings*

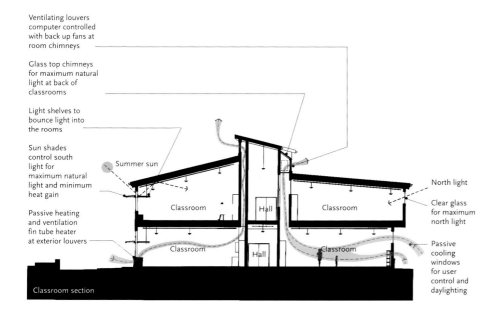

Ventilating louvers computer controlled with back up fans at room chimneys

Glass top chimneys for maximum natural light at back of classrooms

Light shelves to bounce light into the rooms

Sun shades control south light for maximum natural light and minimum heat gain

Passive heating and ventilation fin tube heater at exterior louvers

Summer sun

Classroom

Hall

Classroom

Hall

Classroom

Classroom

North light

Clear glass for maximum north light

Passive cooling windows for user control and daylighting

Classroom section

Every element of a school building can provoke learning for those within it. By designing sustainable systems, we support our children's future well-being along with their daily education. By exposing the inner workings of a building, we give students grist for inquiry wherever they look.

Daylighting and natural ventilation are important for the comfort of the school's occupants.

At left: Existing trees from the building site were salvaged to compose this school's grand pillars.

Widely various design strategies exist to develop more sustainable buildings. In general, they fall into approaches that concern site development, water efficiency, energy use, material and resource use, and indoor environmental quality. Strategies such as proper daylighting and natural ventilation can demonstrate connections to our surrounding environments, save construction money by downsizing electrical and mechanical systems, and generate long-term cost savings by using less energy. Visible building systems that conserve energy and use water efficiently can also help students understand the local, regional, and global interconnections of ecosystems.

This building's vegetated roof and natural vegetation system reflect the school's commitment to the environment.

Solar panels allow schools to be responsible community buildings. At the same time, students can explore alternative energy options right at their school.

Almost every design element can contribute to a growing awareness of interconnectedness by students, teachers, and the community. Inquiry and analysis can grow out of simple observations: the placement of a window bringing daylight deep into a classroom; the composition of a floor utilizing recycled material; the flow of water through a cleansing bio-swale before release into regional storm water pipes; the digital control of a heating system that captures heat from stale, discharged air as an efficient method of pre-heating fresh supply air. Exposing to the eye the building's systems – its structural supports, heating ducts, water pipes, electrical conduit, wiring for information systems – invites everyone to think about them and ask questions. Whether those questions result in engineering projects, mathematical cost-benefit analysis, or research into environmental law, they have value far beyond the moment.

▶ **IN PRACTICE**

Think of both present responsibilities and future opportunities while applying sustainable design principles to a new or existing facility. Explore strategies that make visible the system of a living building to provoke inquiry and understanding among those who learn there.

Exposing a building's structural and mechanical systems
is both cost effective and stimulating – the building and its
systems can be used as teaching tools.

Architects of Achievement focuses on building bridges between educational design and architecture. Bringing knowledge of brain research, effective teaching methods, and sound educational facilities design, they help school districts, foundations, government agencies, charter organizations, and architectural firms think creatively about design solutions capable of fostering higher achievement for all.

Our work has been featured in *Architecture Magazine, Architectural Record, Edutopia, The American School Board Journal,* and *School Planning and Management Magazine* and by the Knowledge Works Foundation, the Rural School and Community Trust, Stanford's School Redesign Network, Small Schools Northwest at Lewis and Clark College, the Coalition of Essential Schools, the Colorado Children's Campaign, the Council of Educational Facilities Planners International, the Small Schools Project, and the Bill & Melinda Gates Foundation.

Architects of Achievement is an educational consulting firm, not a licensed architectural firm.

Victoria Bergsagel is an educator passionate about designing schools where all students achieve. Harvard-educated, Victoria has been a teacher, principal, adjunct professor, community relations director, and school district administrator. As Director of Educational Design in a large school district, she led the educational program planning upon which the construction of new schools was based. A creative thinker who brings an unrelenting advocacy for kids and a vast knowledge of educational research, she has also served as a Director of Educational Partnerships at Talaris Research Institute, where she worked with researchers and educators to conduct, integrate, and interpret the world's leading brain research. She founded and directs Architects of Achievement and has a gift for nurturing people's talents and insights to arrive at inspired solutions. Two of her projects (Todd Beamer High School and the Truman Educational Complex) have been finalists for the James D. MacConnell Award – the highest honor in school planning and design given annually to one project somewhere in the world by the Council of Education Facility Planners International, the largest and oldest international school planning organization. Balancing work with a love of the arts and outdoors, Victoria is a connoisseur of fine opera, extreme ski slopes, and Northwest bike trails.

Tim Best is a strategic adviser experienced in envisioning and implementing projects focused on change, technology, and learning. In addition to his work with Architects of Achievement, he directs MATRIX Learning, a national project conducting research on the application of informal learning strategies that happen with games and mobile technologies to middle school math. Tim is also the Director of State Partnerships at the Wexford Institute (CA) and directs catalystOHIO, a partnership of fifty universities for the Ohio Board of Regents. As a policymaker, Tim established and directed Ohio SchoolNet, a state agency that distributed over $800 million for educational technology to Ohio schools, ultimately wiring over 100,000 classrooms. He was the first executive director of the Center for Leadership in Education, a Cleveland-based foundation focused on school change, and served as the Director of Advanced Development at Fitch, Inc., a London-based design consultancy specializing in retail spaces and learning environments.

Kathleen Cushman has written for over twenty years about the lives and learning of adolescents. From 1988 to 2001 she documented the work of high school change around the country, during which time she helped found the Francis W. Parker Charter Essential School in Devens, Massachusetts. In 2000 she co-founded the nonprofit organization What Kids Can Do, Inc., where she works directly with youth around the nation to make public their voices and views. Cushman is the author of *Fires in the Bathroom: Advice for Teachers from High School Students* (New Press, 2003); *Sent to the Principal: Students Talk About Making High Schools Better* (Next Generation Press, 2005), and *First in the Family: Advice About College from First-Generation Students* (Next Generation Press, 2005, 2006). Among many other books, she co-authored *Learning and the Real World* (Jossey-Bass, 1999) and *The Real Boys Workbook* (Random House, 2001). Her writings on high school change appear in five volumes as *The Collected Horace: Theory and Practice of Essential Schools* (Coalition of Essential Schools, 1998). Her fiction, poems, and essays have appeared in many national publications, including the *Atlantic*, the *New Yorker*, and the *New York Times Magazine*. When not on the road, she lives in New York City.

Lorne McConachie is a senior principal architect with Bassetti Architects in Seattle, Washington, focused on the design of engaging public places. Over the past twenty-five years, he has developed extensive expertise in the programming and design of educational facilities and is recognized as a gifted facilitator of interactive planning processes to achieve a common vision. His designs have won acclaim for their innovation, impact on learning, and civic and design excellence. They range from embedding a small high school in Seattle Center, the city's cultural hub, to reconstructing historic schools to meet the educational needs of twenty-first-century learners. His Edmonds-Woodway High School design captured the 1999 James D. MacConnell Award, and in 2004 his Todd Beamer High School design was a finalist for the same award. Beyond his passion for design, Lorne can be found playing baseball, hiking the trails of the Pacific Northwest, or exploring an old building in his commitment to historic preservation.

Wendy Sauer believes that when challenged, engaged, and supported, students excel. Wendy's passion for education and acute understanding of educational issues was honed through a decade in the classroom and a master's degree in curriculum and instruction. As director of education at Experience Music Project, Wendy prepared materials and professional development opportunities aimed at using popular music to engage students in core academics. In this capacity, she directed the development of the acclaimed teachers guide for the PBS series "The Blues." A graduate of the University of California, Berkeley, Wendy has consulted with a variety of educational organizations, including the Library of Congress, and is a recipient of the prestigious James Madison Fellowship. On Sunday mornings, Wendy can be found, coffee in hand, building fairy castles and singing with her two daughters, Ella and Halle.

David Stephen is an architect whose professional life straddles the worlds of architecture and education reform. As an architect, he has over twenty years of experience in building design and construction. As an education reformer, he has worked with high schools nationwide to envision, develop, and implement innovative practices in teaching and learning. In addition to his work with Architects of Achievement, David is a co-founder and the Design Director of High Tech High (HTH), the nationally acclaimed charter school in San Diego, California. HTH runs a California-based network of charter schools that adhere both programmatically and architecturally to the HTH design principles of personalization, coherent intellectual mission, and adult-world connection. The HTH facility received a 2001 Educational Design Excellence Award from the American School and University Architectural Portfolio. Both the HTH and High Tech Middle facilities have received Honors Awards from the School Construction News and Design Share Awards, in 2002 and 2003 respectively. David received his Bachelors of Architecture degree from Rhode Island School of Design, and his Masters of Education from Lesley College. When not traveling the country working with schools, he enjoys spending time with his family, hiking in the Vermont woods, and salsa dancing.

IMAGE CREDITS

Bassetti Architects: 26 (*bottom*), 89, 102, 140, 141, 149

Benjamin Benschneider, Courtesy of Mahlum Architects: 144

Victoria Bergsagel: Cover (*top*), 9, 14, 16, 22, 23, 24, 27, 30, 31 (*bottom*), 37, 46-47, 51, 52, 59, 61, 62, 64, 66, 68, 69, 70, 71, 72, 75, 76, 78, 79, 80, 81, 85, 86, 91, 105, 110, 112, 125, 128, 129, 134, 136, 150

Tim Best: 44 (*top*), 82, 98-99

Travis Culwell: 74, 95

DLR Group Architects: 25, 34, 119

From the Collections of The Henry Ford Museum: 88, 118

Art Grice, Courtesy of Bassetti Architects: 26 (*top*), 29 (*top*), 94

HMC Architects: 31 (*top*), 67 (*right*)

Cheri Hendricks: 87

James F. Housel, Courtesy of Bassetti Architects: 42, 49

Ellis Kaufman: 28, 57

Mahlum Architects: 108 (*bottom*), 124

Lorne McConachie, Bassetti Architects: 32, 145, 146

Bill Robinson, Courtesy of High Tech High: 60, 77, 80

James Steinkamp, Courtesy of Perkins + Will Architects: 48, 117; Courtesy of OWP/P Architects: 50

Wendy Sauer: 44 (*bottom*)

David Stephen: 29 (*bottom*), 35, 36, 38, 41 (*colorization*), 45, 54, 55 (*top*), 58, 67 (*left*), 73, 84, 90 (*right*), 101, 103, 104, 106, 108 (top), 111, 116, 118 (*colorization*), 121, 123 (*top*), 130, 131, 132, 135, 137, 151

Kevin Veatch: Cover (*main*), 6, 10, 11, 13, 20-21, 33, 43, 53, 55 (*bottom*), 56, 83, 90 (*left*), 93, 96, 100, 107, 109, 110, 114-115, 120, 122, 123 (*bottom*), 126-127, 133, 139, 142, 143, 147, 148, 151

WLC Architects: 41